HELL ALERT

HELL ALERT

Gary H. Murray &
S. Charles Murray

Lifesource Publishing
Atlanta, Georgia

For inquiries or comments regarding this book, or for information about special discounts for bulk purchases, please contact:

Lifesource Publishing
P. O. Box 54982
Atlanta, Georgia 30308
www.LifesourcePublishing.com

The term "mankind," drawn from Biblical language, is employed in this book to represent humanity as a whole, both males and females.

This publication includes verses from King James Version (KJV) of the Bible; the Amplified Bible, Classic Edition (AMPC); and the New International Version (NIV) of the Bible.

Cover and interior book design: Creative Publishing Book Design
www.creativepublishingdesign.com

First paperback edition October 2023

Manufactured in the United States of America

Publisher's Cataloging-in-Publication data

Names: Murray, Gary H., author. | Murray, S. Charles, author.
Title: Hell alert / Gary H. Murray & S. Charles Murray
Description: Atlanta, GA: Lifesource Publishing, 2023.
Identifiers: LCCN: 2023918233 | ISBN: 979-8-218-28651-4
Subjects: LCSH: Hell--Christianity. | Hell--Biblical teaching. | Faith. | Christianity. | Christian life. | BISAC: RELIGION / Christian Living / General | RELIGION / Christian Living / Afterlife | RELIGION / Christian Living / Inspirational
Classification: LCC BT836.3 .M87 2023 | DDC 236/.25--dc23

*This book is dedicated to
our wonderful children and grandchildren
and all our amazing nieces and nephews.*

*We also dedicate the book, with special thanks, to
Cie Meadows Murray and Linda Murray Jackson
for all their love and support.*

Contents

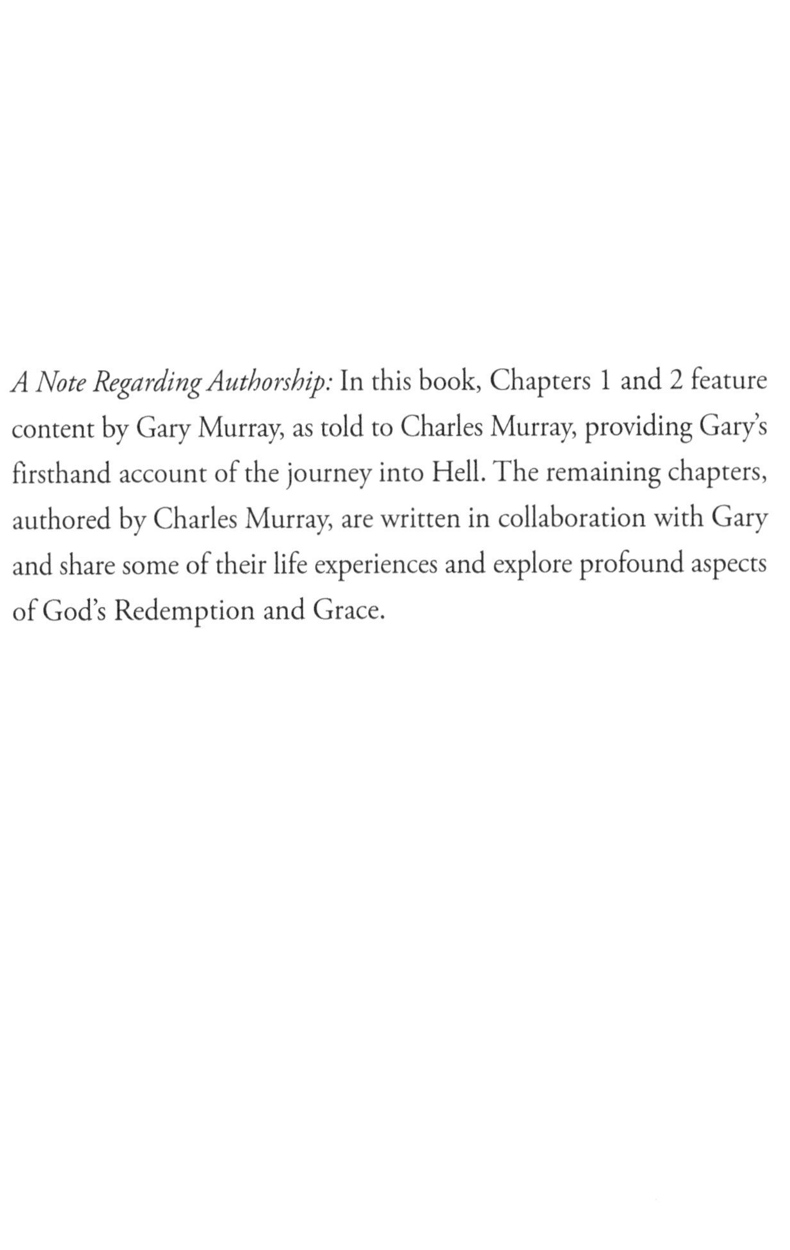

A Note Regarding Authorship: In this book, Chapters 1 and 2 feature content by Gary Murray, as told to Charles Murray, providing Gary's firsthand account of the journey into Hell. The remaining chapters, authored by Charles Murray, are written in collaboration with Gary and share some of their life experiences and explore profound aspects of God's Redemption and Grace.

Introduction

Is there a Hell? If there is, what does it really look like? What does it feel like? Is it as bad as what people say or has been portrayed in books and movies? As a human race, our real concern has got to be: If there *is* a Hell, how do we keep from going there?

Like probably almost everyone on earth, we have thought about where we're going to go when we die and leave this planet. We also ponder other age-old questions: Why was I born? What is my purpose in being here? Where did I/we come from? Not only is it important to ask these questions, but also to honestly seek the answers.

The purpose of this book is not to answer all of these questions. However, our hope is that you will find some answers in the words and experiences we have felt called to share with you here. Don't be surprised if some new questions arise before you reach the end of this book and even after you finish it. We invite you to approach this not with fear, but rather with openness to finding the answers you seek.

In this book, we will share with you real events experienced by a real person and the realities he saw by dying and going to a place beyond and beneath this earth. The Bible calls this place Hell. That person is Gary Murray. Gary is an average person, a regular guy. He's a husband, father, grandfather, brother, and a friend to many. He's my biological brother whom I have known all my life. He is not by any stretch of the imagination extraordinary. So why would God choose him to have this experience? No one knows, not even Gary. I guess God did not need anyone's permission to choose him—He just did.

This story is not a made-for-television science fiction movie or some action thriller for the big screen. It *really* happened! There will be many who will believe these events and, unfortunately, some who will not believe. Despite our knowing that these things happened, our goal in writing this book is not to try to convince you of anything. We only wish to share with you our experiences in the context of God's word, the Holy Bible. *You* are the one who has to decide what you believe.

What is certain is that, for those who will see and hear them, within this story and these words are many examples of God's love, grace, and compassion for mankind. And, most likely, there will be things within our sharing that you can relate to in your own life. Like so many people, we have traveled from a state of unbelief, to misinformation (or just not knowing who God is), to having a deep and life-changing relationship with God, whom we now know as a Father who loves us.

We invite you to take some time to read this book and ask God to help you understand how these stories and words relate to you. We encourage you to share it with others while keeping a copy for yourself as a reference guide for living your life. We pray and trust you will be blessed by it.

Chapter One

Gary's Testimony of Hell

As told by Gary Murray

There I was, in the Veteran Affairs (VA) hospital in Baltimore in June 2013. My home is in Quincy, Florida, a small town approximately twenty miles west of Tallahassee. I had traveled to Maryland to visit my daughter Mary Beth, who lives there. Before arriving in Baltimore, I had been feeling fine. Like most people in their late sixties, I was experiencing my share of aches and pains from just life and living in general, but all in all my health was pretty good.

I had been doing some minor repair work and cleanup around my daughter's house when, afterward, I suddenly fell ill with a tremendous pain in my stomach. After more than an hour, the pain had not gotten any better, no matter what I did for it. My daughter and some others suggested I go to the hospital. I agreed and was driven to the VA, an appropriate place since I am a veteran of the U.S. Marine Corps and served a tour of duty in combat in the war in Vietnam.

Some years before this event, I had been diagnosed with a condition called diverticulitis. I thought maybe this pain I was having had something to do with that. But it turned out to be even more serious. After some examinations, the doctors told me I had an obstruction in my intestinal area. They said it could be a hernia or some type of growth surrounding my large intestine and other vital organs. They said it was life-threatening and required immediate surgery. All the while, I was in immense pain.

Naturally, I was full of fear and anxiety over this news. No one likes to hear that you're going to die if they don't do immediate surgery on you. Yet not even the fear of dying was as bad as what happened next.

I agreed to have the surgery and, while I was lying in my hospital bed, before the surgery or even being given any anesthesia, *I died.*

Even now, just using the word "died" feels strange to me. I know that what I am sharing with you here will be hard for some of you to believe; it is hard enough for me to believe and I lived it. Yet, there is no other word or reality to describe what happened: *I died.*

Then, what happened next changed my life forever. I will describe the events that followed as simply and plainly as I know how to, because nothing like this had ever happened to me before, not even in my wildest dreams or imagination.

Although I was dead, and away from life on earth as I knew it, I continued to exist. I could see. I could hear. I could feel. (Maybe I could touch—I don't know, as there was nothing around me close enough to reach for.) There were feelings of pain, anxiety, and fear all around me. I was experiencing a reality that is just as clear as life is here on this earth, and in many ways, it felt even more real.

Then, I felt myself as what I can only call my spirit and soul depart my physical body. As I was rising up, I looked back and saw my earthly body lying still on the hospital bed. At that point, I felt myself being pulled away, but now in a downward direction.

Suddenly, darkness was all around me. It felt like some Devilish creature had ahold of me and was pulling what now felt like a different "body" I was residing in downward. This body was the same likeness and form of the body I resided in on earth, but it seemed to now be decaying and deformed. I could feel myself moving downward into the earth, surrounded by utter darkness.

It is so difficult to describe the undescribable, but I will do the best I can.

My eyes were open, yet I could see only blackness. All of my senses seemed sharper and heightened. I had a greater sense of smell and of hearing, and even of physical feeling. I could hear and feel pain all around me. I could smell the stench of death everywhere.

All around me was what I can only describe as continuous death or a death that never ended. It was not just my pain I felt; I could sense and feel the pain of so many other souls in that place. I don't know how many were there, but many, many more than I could count. I heard the desperate mourning and pleadings for help and escape of what felt like millions of lost souls.

It was at that point that I realized that this *was not* a dream or some horrible nightmare that I could quickly wake up from. This was *real*. It was a new reality that I now found myself in.

My first thoughts and words to myself (and to God if He was listening) were, *Why am I here? How did I get here? I should not be here, because I am a Christian!* I could never have imagined such a place existed and, if I could have, I certainly would have hoped that I would never end up there.

There was no order, only chaos and confusion. There was so much pain, sickness, disease, and deformity. While I could not observe their physical faces with my eyes, these souls and personalities showed me their *presence,* which was just as visible and clear to me as any physical person I had ever seen with my natural eyes on earth. I had access to new senses in this version of my self (body and soul) that I did not have on earth, which were heightened in this place. They gave me a discernment and ability to know what and who was around me even in the darkness.

To my surprise and heartache, I saw people I recognized from earth—some of whom I thought for sure would have been in Heaven. There were prominent people who had held important titles and positions on earth. There were church people and even people who were saying they had been a preacher or minister. Many were yelling out the positions they had held while they were alive. I heard them crying in pain and agony, all the while I wondered, "How did they get here?" And, "Why am *I* here?"

I repeated those words to myself over and over again, "Why am I here?" I was so afraid. I cried aloud to the top of my voice, "I am not supposed to be here!" I repeated, "I am a Christian. I am saved. I am not supposed to be here." But it made no difference. It did not change my condition. I remained in Hell just like all the other lost souls there.

How could this be? I thought, *I'm a good person. Yes, I made mistakes in my life, but nothing so bad as to deserve this agony.*

If you think you have any idea what Hell is like, believe me, you don't. There are not words in the human language or any feelings that you or I or any other human being has ever experienced on earth to describe the torment of Hell. All I can say is that I pray you never go there and that I will never go there again.

In Hell, the souls would cry and scream all the time and at the top of their voices for some relief, and yet no one was available to help. In Hell, no one cares about anyone else; their only concern is to get some relief from their own pain and torment. And then there were the tormentors, the demons whose job it was to inflict the pain of torment on the people in Hell. How heartless and cruel they are.

"Why is all this here? Why is this place necessary?" you are left asking yourself. Then it finally hits you: "So *this* is the punishment for the sin of making the wrong choice on earth."

During my experience in Hell, I heard people saying things like, "I was a good person," "I don't deserve this," "I'm sorry and I repent," and "God, just give me another chance!" All to no avail. It was too late. I realized that there is only one right choice, and that choice needed to be made back then, while we are alive on earth in the physical body.

Then it dawned on me that I *had* made the right choice on earth. I'm not sure how long I had been in Hell at that moment, but I suddenly realized that the right choice I had made on earth was that I had accepted Jesus as my Lord and Savior. I *knew* I had accepted Jesus as my Lord and Savior while I was on earth. So I too began to scream out at the top of my voice, "*Jesus, Jesus, Jesus!* You know I am not supposed to be here. You are my Lord and Savior, and God is my Father. *I am not supposed to be here!*"

Immediately, my circumstances began to change. I felt relief and the presence of the Lord Jesus Himself. There was a Heavenly host that came to lift me out, and I felt myself ascending out of that place. Up and up I went, in the same motion that I'd come down. I was conscious and aware. It was a reality that was as real as anything I have ever experienced on earth.

I was so overjoyed and happy. No experience you have ever had or will ever have could be more wonderful. The feeling was the greatest joy and most intense relief over being freed from the captivity and bondage of Hell. *I am out of Hell!* went through my mind. I was also asking God how it was possible that I got there. I wanted to know, because I did not want to ever go back. But all I could say now was, "Thank you, Jesus!"

The next very strange thing that happened was where I arrived when I got back to earth. As I said earlier, I live in Quincy, Florida. After leaving this Hell place, I did not immediately arrive back at the VA hospital. I found myself instead in my hometown of Quincy, at night and alone, in the middle of the football field of my old high school, called Carter-Parramore High School. I don't know if I was physically there, but I do know that everything around me was familiar and comfortable. I don't know why or how I got there. And I did not and still do not know the significance of God returning me to my old school. I guess God just wanted me to be in a place that was known to me even as a child. The school and field looked the same way they did when I was a student there. While I never played organized football, the stadium was a place I had spent a lot of time attending games. I think God just knew this setting would represent the real earth to me when I got back. To me, it didn't matter where I was or how I got there; I was just so grateful to be back on this earth and out of the doom and darkness of the Hell I had experienced.

Soon after my high school football stadium arrival experience, I found myself back in the VA hospital room in Baltimore, surrounded by several doctors and nurses. They were looking at me as though I had been unconscious for some time, but not very much time had passed at all. At least not much time in the natural earthly sense. They then explained, "You were yelling and screaming. Why? Are you okay?" I didn't ask them how long I was screaming. I just supposed, as I did not really want to know.

My experience of Hell shook me to the very core of my being. The people in the hospital room probably thought I had lost my mind. If I had not personally experienced it, I would have thought so too. But, again, this was not a dream or even some terrible nightmare. I have had dreams and nightmares before, and this was nothing like any of them. This was not a delusion or some mind lapse. I don't know why, but God let me see into the very darkness of Hell. And He let me return to share with those who will listen about this real place of unspeakable, intense torment and horror. Still, I ask God, "Why me? Who do I tell, and will anyone believe me?"

I get no joy from sharing this with you. In fact, it has taken me nearly ten years to put this story into book form. I have tried to forget about it and make the thoughts go away. But they simply will not. God said to tell the story because the world needs to be reminded. There are many who will believe, and others who will not. Our assignment (my brother's and mine) is to tell of my experience and to share a message of life and hope in God through our Lord and Savior Jesus Christ, which we trust you will find in this book.

Chapter Two

Why Did God Choose Us?

"For God hath chosen the foolish things of the world to confound the wise; and God hath chosen the weak things of the world to confound the things which are mighty."
—*1 Corinthians 1:27 (KJV)*

From Gary

God Chose Me

Since my experience of going to Hell, my story has been met with many different reactions from the people I have shared this experience with. These range from "I believe" and complete amazement to almost total disbelief, saying, "How can this be?" The question I am most often asked, however, is, "Why you? Of all people, why would God choose *you* to have such an experience?" The next most popular question is, "If you did go to Hell, how did you really get out?"

The honest answer to the first question is: I don't know why God chose me. And the truth about how I got out is: I got out because of Jesus. I don't know how exactly, but when I called on Jesus, I was simply taken out. After much time of reflection, I know that while on earth and before going to Hell, I had accepted Jesus as my Lord and Savior. I was born again. I knew based on God's promise, I should not be in Hell. That is why I kept saying, "Why am I here? I shouldn't be here."

Believe me, over the years, I have asked the Lord these and many other questions about this experience. And I have not always gotten the answers I wanted or expected. Once, God led me to the Scripture in 1 Corinthians 1:27 (KJV): "God hath chosen the foolish things of the world to confound the wise, and God hath chosen the weak things of the world to confound the things which are mighty."

What I do know is that this experience changed my life. It has given me a second chance to get some things right that I was getting wrong in life. One of those things is how I see people and treat people. I was not always kind to people, but I am getting better. I have not completely arrived, but I am working on it and continue to get better in that arena. Few people on this planet are given the chance to live after seeing what's on the other side of death. I have been given the gift of coming back to share that experience with the world. Maybe that is the reason for the experience. God wants me to share this experience with others in hopes that they will believe in Him, accept Jesus Christ as their Lord and Savior, and avoid Hell.

From Charles

My Brother, My Friend, My Family

I have known Gary all of my life. I am Charles Murray, Gary's younger brother. We grew up together in a family of ten children in a small rural community in northwest Florida called Greensboro. There were seven sons and three daughters from the union of our parents, Roseanna and Joseph Murray. Gary is the sixth son, and I am the seventh.

Our parents were working-class people. We often struggled to get by and were in the range of what I would call a lower-to-moderate income family. If we really met the definition of poor, I could not tell it. As a child, I felt loved because we lived in a happy home. Most families in the neighborhood were like us, so our financial condition felt normal. All of us kids knew our parents were doing the best they could to support and take care of their family.

Gary is almost nine years older than me. Since there was such a gap in our ages, we had different friends growing up and really didn't hang out together much. But we always got along well and I always respected and admired him. After high school, Gary pursued a career path that meant joining the Marine Corps, which included a tour in Vietnam. I was in middle school and high school when Gary was away in the military.

When I graduated from high school, I too left home and went away to college. From there, our lives continued to take us down separate paths with different interests and pursuits. Yet, even while in different places, Gary and I always stayed in touch, by talking on the telephone and seeing each other occasionally. Later in our lives, we became closer. I supposed we both just matured more. Now, Gary is my best friend. We are now not only biological brothers, but we are also connected in the most important way, we are spiritual brothers in the Lord Jesus Christ.

We grew up in a Christian home and a loving environment. Both of our parents were caring and nurturing people. They both came from a big family themselves, so it seemed natural for them to want to have a big family of their own. My mother had eleven siblings and my father had six. I did not know my father, as I was only a year-and-a-half old when he died tragically in a work-related accident at the age of forty-seven.

Much of what I know about him, I learned from my mother and my older brothers and sisters. I know he was a good man and that he loved God, even though he did not go to church very much. I had heard from my siblings that something or someone turned Dad off to church and church folk. Mom found it almost impossible to convince him to attend church during their marriage. I never knew exactly the reason that Daddy didn't go to church. I think the family all accepted it as just the way it was. What I did learn from the family and others who knew Daddy well was that he frequently read the Bible and knew Scriptures and could often quote them.

When it came to going to church and the things of God, Mom was just the opposite. She went to church every time she could. She saw to it that all of her children went to church and even Sunday school, at least when we were young and she could control us. She was an amazing influence on all of us. Her love for the things of God kept the family together, especially in hard times.

From what I was told about Daddy, I could see that Gary was a lot like him, especially when they both were younger. They both were very adventurous and loved a challenge. Both served in the United States military: Dad in the Navy and Gary in the Marine Corps. They both loved working with their hands and to build and grow things. Dad always had gardens and fruit trees, and he even helped build the home that we grew up in. Gary is the same way still. He always has a building project, a vegetable garden, or is raising animals like chickens, ducks, pigs, and goats. I know we all took on some of our parents' qualities, but those shared between Dad and Gary seem most similar and striking to me.

Gary was certainly not very different from the rest of us. He was a bit more adventurous and seemed to always be able to find some kind of trouble to get into. But there was nothing special or extraordinary about him. Certainly nothing obvious about him, in my judgment, that would cause him to be chosen by God to have an experience of Hell. After lots of reflection on it, we are both still left with the question: Why him?

An Amazing Connection

When Gary first shared with me his experience of going to Hell, I immediately believed him. He told me that I was the first person he had spoken to in detail about this event. I know him well enough to know that he could never have made up anything so amazing and extraordinary. The details and descriptions were so graphic and real. In our entire lives, Gary and I had never had a conversation even remotely similar to the one about his Hell experience. Yes, Gary's description of such a dark reality could only have come from a real experience in the pits of Hell itself. The emotional impact and burdensome toll it took on Gary was unlike anything I have ever seen him go through before. When he first told me about it, his voice was literally shaking and he was almost without words. Gary was a totally changed person after this experience.

It was soon after his Hell experience that he called me. I remember I was at work sitting in my office when I saw his name appear on my cell phone. Somehow, even before he called me, I had a sense that something was going on with him. I knew he had traveled to Baltimore to see his daughter, but I did not know about the emergency hospital visit until his call. When we talked, I could sense that he was emotionally and mentally shaken. And as he explained things to me, I understood quickly that he had gone through some kind of traumatic experience.

As I sat there listening to him, I was speechless. I believed him, but I simply did not know what to say to him at that moment. All I could do is to sit there and listen to a mortal man try to explain having just experienced a supernatural event. As I listened to Gary, I silently asked God, "Lord, what do you want me to do with this information I am hearing?" I thought, *I am his brother, I know that. But why am I the first person he has called to share this experience with? What am I supposed to do with this literally out-of-this-world revelation of Hell experience I am hearing?* I had read about and heard about other people having similar accounts, but I had never known anyone who actually experienced going to Hell and returned back to earth to talk about it. *Who would believe Gary's story?* I got no immediate answer to any of these questions, but somehow, I knew that God would reveal to Gary and me what we were supposed to do and say about it. I just sat there and listened as he shared it with me. My life too was forever changed by the experience.

Sometimes, We Have to Wait

Have you ever had to wait for something that you really wanted a lot? I think all of us have, and sometimes waiting is hard to do. If you are anything like me, you hate waiting, and I don't do it very patiently. I remember as a small child just waiting for Christmas. Not only was it waiting the whole year for that one special day to come back around, but it was also waiting the night before Christmas Day. I could never sleep because of the anticipation of Christmas morning. I was always so happy on Christmas morning, just experiencing the joy of finding and opening the gifts for me under the Christmas tree.

Life is that way. Sometimes we have to wait for those things we really want. Things don't always come immediately or when we want them. That wait is usually part of life's process in getting us where we need to be in order to get us what we want and need in this life. God makes us wait sometimes because that thing we may want may not be the right thing for us or we may not be ready for it at the time. God may make us wait sometimes because, what we are seeking, we may not be spiritually mature enough to handle. The Bible reminds us, "Wait on the Lord, be of good courage, and he shall strengthen thine heart: wait, I say, on the Lord" (Psalm 27:14 KJV). Waiting on God's timing may sometimes be a tough thing for us, but it is never a bad thing. God's timing is always the right timing.

It was years before Gary or I realized that we were supposed to share Gary's Hell experience in a book form. Sure, Gary had all along been telling his experience to different people individually. I think we both knew we needed to do something more. We knew at the beginning that we were supposed to share this story with others. It was Gary who first sensed this—after all, it was his experience. Even though that meant taking the chance that people would not believe us or reject it altogether, we both knew that somehow we needed to step out on what God wanted us to do. Yet God was patient with us, and that meant that a time of waiting and maturing on our parts was needed to better understand how and what to share and who to share it with.

I remember Gary saying to me many times, "Brother, it was real. It really happened. But I don't know why." Gary readily admitted that he did not think he was called to be a preacher and that he was not even that much of a spiritual person. He would say, "I am just a person who loves the Lord and who has been a Christian since my childhood." He went on to say that he never felt very special in God's eyes. I reminded him that we are all special in God's eyes.

You don't have to be some prominent or special person according to the world's standards for God to use you. In fact, God almost always uses people for His glory who are not well-known or even popular. The Bible tells us that God used a person named Saul who was a murderer and persecutor of the Christian church. Saul's name was later changed to the Apostle Paul, and it was he who ended up writing nearly two-thirds of the New Testament and, in doing so, changed the history of the world.

Gary is not the Apostle Paul, but in God's sight, Gary is loved just as Paul was loved by God, and even as Jesus is loved by God. Because, as the Bible tells us, if you have made Jesus the Lord of your life, God has called you and sees you as His son or daughter just like Jesus. In fact, God then sees you as a joint heir with Jesus (Romans 8:17).

For me, this period of waiting lasted more than eight years from the time Gary shared his story of Hell with me to the time we were inspired to share his story with a wider audience by writing this book. These eight years have truly been a time of maturing for me. I believe I have gotten closer to God and have gotten to know His Will and Plans for my life better. Indeed, God has a plan or plans for me and not just for me, but for all of us humans. We have to discover it and begin to walk and operate in it. God tells us in Jeremiah 29:11 (AMPC), "For I know the thoughts and plans that I have for you, says the Lord, thoughts and plans for welfare and peace and not for evil, to give you hope in your final outcome." Over time, I have learned how to better hear from God and to better appreciate the importance of obeying His Word in order to know what He wants me to do with my life.

During this eight-year journey, I have learned that getting to know God better requires going to the source. The source is, of course, God's Word—the Holy Bible. I accept the Holy Bible as the inspired Word of God. It is there in the Bible that I first went looking for answers to, "Is there really a Hell? When there are so many other, nicer things to talk about, why was Gary given this Hell experience and why does God want us to talk about it?" Before I could talk about it, I first needed to study and examine for myself if this Hell was a real place. Needless to say, I did not want the experience of going there like Gary before I talked about it. So I asked God for His help.

Chapter Three

Is Hell a Real Place?

The questions that nearly every living human being at some time in their life has or will ask themselves are: *Is there really a Hell? And, if so, is Hell a real place?* Some people have asked me, "How can you be so sure there is a Hell if you have never seen it?" I usually respond by saying, "I have never seen my brain, but I am pretty sure I've got one." There are just some things you know because your senses and your intuitive nature recognize the truth in it. I am a Believer in the Bible as the Word of God, and the Bible tells us that there is a Hell. Therefore, I recognize and believe it to be true. Guessing and wondering about whether Hell exists is not a question whose answer you want to get wrong. My source is the Holy Bible. The Bible calls God the Creator of the Universe. Who should know better than God if there is a Hell? The Bible mentions the word "Hell" or a variation of it over seventy times.

Like Gary's experience in Hell, I am aware from research that God has allowed a limited number of people to experience what Hell is like and then come back to share their experiences with the world. There have been other books written about Hell and perhaps many other real examples of the Hell experience never written down. Gary's experience in Hell almost did not get written down and shared. It was only by the prompting of the Holy Spirit that we became inspired to write this book.

Our primary hesitation and pause in sharing Gary's story was our concern about who would believe it. After years of prayer, hearing, and maturing more in God's Word, we became clear that it was not our business or job to concern ourselves with who believed. It was only our responsibility to get the message out. It was God's job to handle the people-believing part.

People often define Hell in very loose terms. The world regularly makes references like "I'm having a hell of a day," "I'm in a living hell," and "This is Hell on earth." Other people ask, "How can there be any place worse than what I am going through here on earth?" Little do they know that there is indeed a place a million times worse than anything they can ever experience here in this realm.

I remember when I was a little boy about five or six years old. I would have these terrible nightmares that caused me to wake up in the middle of the night. I would see myself being chased by some evil person or creature I thought was the Devil. I'm sure many children have these kinds of dreams. Yet it was especially frightening to me because I had no one to explain what it meant and why the nightmares were happening.

I heard stories from family and friends and watched horror movies on television and developed my own ideas of what or who the Devil is. I knew that the Devil and Hell were bad. I got this from some things I read in school and in books and heard from my preacher and my Sunday school teacher at church. I heard enough and knew enough to not want to go there. However, I never thought too much about it. Looking back, I suppose I hoped it was not real and just tried to put these kinds of thoughts out of my mind. Being young, this just wasn't cool or any fun to think about. I had many more other things in life to think about that would make me happy.

However, as I grew up, I began to realize that the life we live on this earth has many realities. The most obvious reality is that, as human beings, we all live and we all die. So, we must all examine the question of where we go when we die. Is there an afterlife? Is there a Hell? It is certainly not like my nightmares. As bad as those nightmares were, things were okay when I woke up. Tragically, you don't get to wake up from a death sentence to Hell.

Although it may not seem like it, the purpose of these words and this book is not to frighten you and leave you without hope. The purpose of this book is actually to inform and enlighten you, cause you to stop and think, and help you make some vital choices about how you live your life on earth and where you choose to live in eternity. Our intent is to make you aware that there is life after death and there is a destination for you after you leave this earth. We want to help you realize that you have more of a choice in where you go when you leave the earth than you might think.

What Does the Bible Say about Hell?

As a Christian and a Believer, I first look to the Holy Bible as my spiritual authority. The word "Hell" or its variations (Hades, Sheol, the Lower World, the place of the Dead) are mentioned over seventy times in the Bible. If Hell was not a real place, why would it be addressed so many times in the Bible? God wants us to know about Hell but He does not want all of our attention placed on it. Like Hell, Heaven is also a real place, and it is mentioned in the Bible over five hundred times. God obviously wants our attention to be more on His desired destination for mankind—Heaven. But let there be no mistake, Hell is a real place. If it were not so, God would have told us in His Word, the Bible.

The Bible defines Hell as a place for the dead (Proverbs 9:18). Hell is a separation from God. It is described as a place of fire and brimstone and eternal torment (Matthew 5:22, 23:33). Hell was not a place originally designed for mankind. It is a place that was reserved for Satan and his angels, sons of disobedience, and his demonic forces. Hell is a choice, and choosing to go to Hell is a decision each man and woman can make. Hell is your choice by denying Jesus and not accepting Him as your Lord and Savior.

So, then, many will ask, "If Hell is such a bad place, why would God let us go there? If God is such a good and merciful God, wouldn't He do something to help us or at least warn us about Hell?" The answer is very simple. God gives all of us warning signs all the time about our bad choices, including Hell. For example, God may send a friend or family member by your home to tell you that you shouldn't do this or that thing. You may get a gentle prompting in your conscience, also known as your spirit, to go in a certain direction or follow a certain path. God has countless ways to help us. The question is, are you listening and paying attention to the warning signs?

God has done something about Hell. God loves mankind so much that He gives us all a choice. He does not make us or force us to do anything. He has given us all the choice of where we get to spend eternity. We call this choice "free will." I know it is hard to believe that God will give us *free will* and a free choice because, when we think of God, we think of Him in human terms. So many see God as overbearing or some kind of tyrant, and not as a Loving Father. Mankind does not see God as the Divine, supernatural, and Loving Being that He is. God is not the human being in the flesh-body neighbor next door, or your coworker, or even your cousin Joe; God is a Holy Presence, a Loving and Divine Creator and Caretaker who genuinely wants to be your Father if you will let Him.

God has given us the ability to make our own choices about how we live our life and even how we die—and where we go when we die. However, God does not just give us the choice; He encourages us to make the right choice. In one of my favorite Scriptures from the Old Testament, God tells us, "I call heaven and earth to witness this day against you that I have set before you life and death, the blessings and the curses; therefore choose life, that you and your descendants may live" (Deuteronomy 30:19 AMPC). The choices are clearly laid out before us, blessings or curses and life or death. But just in case you don't know or somehow are confused about which to choose, God gives us a little help, indeed a helpful hint, CHOOSE LIFE. Choosing life is simply choosing Jesus, whom God sent to save mankind.

While life and eternal life with God should be the only choice for mankind, God will never make anyone choose Him. As free moral agents, the choice is always ours individually. No one else can make the decision for each of us. We have to decide for ourselves. *You* have to decide for *yourself*. And it is very important that we do have free will to make our own decision. God wants us to want

Him; He does not want us forced into submitting to Him. What a wonderful place Heaven must be because those who are there are the ones who chose to make Jesus their Lord and Savior and Heaven their ultimate home.

Did God Warn Us about Hell in the Bible?

"Has God *really* warned us about Hell as a consequence to our choices on earth?" you might ask. The answer is yes. He has warned us about Hell many times over. God has warned us throughout the Bible that Hell is a real place. He has also given us apostles, prophets, teachers, evangelists, and pastors to show us, teach us, and explain to us the truth through what is called ministry gifts. The real questions for all of us must be, are we taking the time to listen to these messages and do we believe them?

One of the most powerful and graphic messages about Hell is found in the Gospel of Luke 16:19-31 (KJV). This is the story of Lazarus and the rich man. Here Jesus starts the story by telling us there was a "certain" rich man. When the word "certain" is used in the Bible, it implies the event was an actual event—a true occurrence—not just a story or parable.

19. There was a certain rich man, which was clothed in purple and fine linen, and fared sumptuously every day: 20. And there was a certain beggar named Lazarus, which was laid at his gate, full of sores; 21. And desiring to be fed with the crumbs which fell from the rich man's table: moreover, the dogs came and licked his sores. 22. And it came to pass, that the beggar died, and was carried by the angels in

Abraham's bosom: the rich man also died, and was buried; 23. And in hell he lift up his eyes, being in torments, and seeth Abraham afar off, and Lazarus in his bosom. 24. And he cried and said, Father Abraham, have mercy on me, and send Lazarus, that he may dip the tip of his finger in water, and cool my tongue; for I am tormented in this flame. 25. But Abraham said, Son, remember that thou in thy lifetime receivedst thy good things, and likewise Lazarus evil things: but now he is comforted, and thou are tormented. 26. And beside all this, between us and you there is a great gulf fixed: so that they which would pass from hence to you cannot; neither can they pass to us, that would come from thence. 27. Then he said, I pray thee therefore, father that thou wouldest send him to my father's house: 28. For I have five brethren; that he may testify unto them, lest they also come into this place of torment. 29. Abraham saith unto him, They have Moses and the prophets; let them hear them. 30. And he said, Nay, father Abraham: but if one went unto them from the dead, they will repent. 31. And he said unto him, If they hear not Moses and the prophets, neither will they be persuaded, though one rose from the dead.

This true story is one of the most compelling accounts in the Bible of what the experience of Hell or Hades is like. It shows us that Hell is real. Unfortunately, there are many who, through ignorance and unbelief, will ignore this and make the decision that results in them going there. This rich man made that choice. When he realized it was the wrong choice and a bad decision, it was too late. He suffered much torment in Hell, and this example is only a glimpse into the pain and torment of what Hell is like. Perhaps the greatest of his torments is the regret in knowing that when he was alive, he could have made the decision not to go there.

In Hell, like the rich man, you will remember and have all of your physical and mental senses. The rich man thought about his five brothers whom he left behind. He wanted to get the word to them not to come to this place, but he was told that there is a great separation between Heaven and Hell, and he cannot cross over or even get a message to his brothers from where he is. He asks that, as an alternative, someone be sent from the dead to speak to his brothers. He is told that they have Moses and the prophets and, if they don't listen to them, they are not very likely to listen to a man from the dead.

Do you believe? Do you understand this story? Will you believe Gary's testimony of his Hell experience? We know that there are some who will refuse to believe. We pray that their hearts will change before it is too late.

Chapter Four

What Will You Believe?

You see, there is a Hell. The evidence is overwhelming and abundantly clear. The only question now is, will you believe? Some would ask, "Why would a Loving God ever put us in such a position where we would have to choose between Heaven and Hell?" Amazingly, it was never God's plan that Hell would be an option for mankind. God's plan was that the human race would live and be like Him. Mankind was created in God's image, to be like God (Genesis 1:26-27).

God's original desire was for mankind (male and female) to have dominion over the earth (Genesis 1:26). His desire was for mankind to rule and reign over earth and its creations and to live in peace and harmony while on earth. That may sound pretty outlandish given all the trouble we see in the world today, like crime, war, hatred, disregard, and distrust among people. The Bible says God is Love (1 John 4:8, 16). The Bible also refers to the "love of God," "love of Jesus Christ," and "God's love" over two dozen times in the New Testament alone. And if you think about it, since God is a God of love, it is only natural that God's desire is for mankind to live in a place of love and serenity like Him. Yet, many people think that God got us in this bad way.

You often hear people say, "God is in control of everything." This leads to thinking that the way things are must be God's fault. However, though this may be a surprise to many, there are some things that God does not control. The one thing He left to us is our own *free will.* As we have discussed, mankind has a choice. God gave mankind the ability to make a choice. It is man who gets to choose to do right or wrong. There are those who don't want to take responsibility for their own actions or wrongdoings. That's because it's much easier to blame God or someone else rather than ourselves for what goes wrong in our life.

It was Adam, the first man God created, who got to make the choice of right or wrong. This man's decision affected the very course of all of human history. (Read the first two chapters of the Book of Genesis.) It was Adam and his wife, Eve, who chose to deviate from God's plan of peace and prosperity by listening to a deceptive voice of the enemy called Satan.

You will see in the Book of Genesis, Satan did not appear openly as himself, but came in a very subtle and conniving way—in the form of a creature (a serpent or snake). This shows us that the enemy will approach us humans in any way or form he can to get our attention and deceive us. His goal is to charm us, con us, and absolutely hoodwink us in any way that he can to get us under his control.

Most often, Satan invades our thought life. Satan's lies try to convince us that we are not good enough, that no one cares about us or likes us, or that we will never make a success of our life. Satan always viciously tries to convince us that these horrible thoughts are our own when they really originate from his own suggestions in our mind.

Satan's ultimate purpose is to destroy all of mankind (John 10:10). Why, you ask? It is because Satan hates God. Satan is jealous of God, and Satan wants to be like God, but he cannot. Satan also hates God's creations, especially mankind. It is because man was made to be like God and made in God's image and likeness (Genesis 1:26-27). Satan wants man to be in Hell in order to control mankind for eternity. Yes, this is real.

Many of you who are reading this know this and believe it. But don't allow yourself to forget and stray or fall away from what you know. I repeat and urge you, please don't stray away from what you know.

Unfortunately, there are also others among you who do not know this and are not sure who or what to believe. Our purpose here is not to make you believe anything, but to share with you that there *is* a right and a wrong, a good and a bad. You must make the correct choice, because your life—your eternal life with God in Heaven—depends on it.

We know it is easy to get comfortable, lazy, and just throw your arms up in the air and say, "This is just too much and I don't want to think about it." BUT DON'T STOP READING THIS BOOK. THERE IS HOPE! Giving up will not change anything because you must know that, no matter how much we may deny it or wish it were not so, there is a destiny and a future we all must face someday.

The enemy wants you defenseless and weak and with no control. There are so many people in that position today, and you may very well be one of them. Maybe that is why you are reading this book. Perhaps it is out of curiosity, or the title caught your attention. I believe that it is no accident that you are reading it, but rather it is by Divine appointment that you are here now.

There is a power and a force that is greater than anything in the Universe. That power is called God's Love. God loves you so much that He will do all that He can to bring you into the Light of His Love. I simply share with you what I know by faith, that there is a relationship that surpasses all understanding and comprehension. That relationship is with God through our Lord Jesus Christ. The choice is yours. We pray you make the right choice.

I Was Not Always Sure or Convinced of What to Believe

Gary and I grew up as young African American males in the small rural southern town of Greensboro, Florida. It's located approximately thirty miles west of Tallahassee. He and I were the youngest of the seven male siblings. Along with our three sisters, there was a total of ten children in our family. From a young age, we were taught by our parents and especially our mother to believe in God and be good Christians. I must admit that I never really understood exactly what it meant to be a good Christian. I just assumed it meant not doing bad things and just staying out of trouble. Most of the time, I really tried hard to do that … I mean to stay out of trouble. But like other kids, we liked playing, hanging out, and just having fun. Honestly, I admit, sometimes a little trouble came my way, and sometimes, I managed to get into it.

My trouble included not obeying Mom's directions sometimes and getting into a few fights from time to time. However, in Gary's case, his trouble was a little different and a bit more intense. Gary at a younger age, and especially in his teen years, would find trouble or maybe the trouble would quite often find him. Gary was a very charismatic young man and leader, so lots of boys in the neighborhood looked up to him and would follow him around. Although he didn't lead a gang, he did have a group of loyal followers of young guys around the community.

I could only observe from a distance because I was too young and Mom would not allow me to be a part of his group. They seemed to be more of a group of adventure seekers than a group of hoodlums trying to get into trouble. However, I do remember some of Gary's activities landing him in the county jail for some minor infraction. After talking to the local sheriff, Mom agreed to let him stay in jail for a few days to teach him a lesson and then bailed him out.

There was this one Sunday when Gary was supposed to be in Sunday school and church, but he and his friends decided to have a pickup football game in an open farm field near our house instead. While trespassing on the field, Gary ended up breaking his leg and had to be taken to the hospital for bandages and a cast. He had to wear the cast for months, which seemed to be the only thing that could slow him down. Needless to say, Mom was very angry, to put it nicely. My trouble was never so exciting as Gary's. I was nine years younger than he was and I guess I just learned from his mistakes or at least discovered how to avoid getting caught. The point of my sharing all this is to show you that we are far from perfect people.

When all of us kids were younger and living in our house, going to church and Sunday school was a *must do*. Mom made it an absolute priority to go to church even when we kids didn't want to. Of course, it became more of a challenge for her to make some of us go as we got older. We mostly went to church because Mom made us rather than because we wanted to go. In my early school years, I often did not understand why I was in church or even what the minister was saying. Like many young people today, there are so many things coming our way, we are not sure what to believe. However, I must admit that I did enjoy other church activities, such as listening to the church choir, seeing my friends, and participating in church dinners, picnics, and field trips.

Even though as a youngster I did not read the Bible very much or understand the church sermons, I still sensed in my heart that being in church was somehow important and special. I could tell somehow that God was starting to set me up for the plan He had for my life. I did not know then, like I know now, that it was the Holy Spirit helping me and guiding me, even at a time when I did not know I needed any help. I know now as an adult that if I had paid attention more and really studied biblical things more, I would have developed my faith at an earlier age. I now encourage parents to train their children in the things of God. This is one of the most important things a parent can do for their children in this life.

So, parents, if you don't know the things of God, I encourage you to get to know Him. Get a Bible or Bible concordances and commentaries. Find a good Christian church that teaches and explains the Word of God. Remember to be selective and discerning about the church you choose to attend, as all churches are not the same. Find a church where the pastor understands and knows how to teach and preach the Word of God. Find a church that loves God and people. Find a church that places the Bible as the top authority, as the truth, and as the inspired Word of God.

Again, *all churches are not the same.* All churches don't believe these things. Avoid ones that don't.

As we all know, there are many distractions in this world we live in. There are so many things vying for our time and attention … and today more than ever before in history. There is television with all of its news reporting, our friends and others we know with their strong opinions and points of view, sports, games, personal hobbies, and all brands of social media, just to name a few.

While this wasn't the case with social media while I was growing up, there were many other attention getters, such as peer pressure, keeping up with Joneses, and just the many doubts of not being good enough to compete with others that go through our minds. This could be especially difficult growing up in a household where there was not much money or financial resources.

Because Mom was a widowed single parent raising ten children, we really struggled financially. The emphasis was only on living, on just getting by. It was hard to convince myself as a kid that spiritual things were important in the big scheme of things, or that God could be depended on to supply my needs.

At that time, I did not know God cared about my needs or even had the time for me, given how busy He must be. I thought, *God's got a lot to do and, no doubt, He is just too busy for me.* It took me many years to find out, and I am still in the process of learning, that God *does* care about me and even the small things that concern me. God cares about where I live, where I sleep, what I eat, what I think about, and who I spend my time with. God even cares when I am happy or sad, and He wants me to be happy. What a thrill to know we have a Loving Father like that.

Who or What Is Influencing Your Beliefs?

You may not always realize it, but there are many things in this life that influence what you think and believe. The greatest factor influencing what you believe is what or who you are exposed to or spend your time around. What you spend your time watching, observing, reading, and being entertained by will certainly influence how you think and behave. Your actions and exposures settle into your subconscious, your human spirit, and influence who you are and who you become.

For example, if you spend most of your time watching certain kinds of movies, you will develop an affinity for those kinds of movies. If you hang out with people who routinely use bad language and do bad things, you too will instinctively adopt those same patterns of using bad words, doing bad things, and likely getting into trouble. Just think about it: All that you are now is a product of the environment you have been exposed to, which includes the people you spend your time with.

Our main and first sources of influence are our parents, teachers, and other adult figures, as well as our peers who are around us when we are children. From the time we are an infant, to a toddler, and then a young adult, we hear and listen to the things older people impart to us. Most of what we learn from well-meaning adults is good and necessary. When I was a kid, I learned from older people how to read and write, how to tie my shoes, and how to play baseball. These and a seemingly infinite number of other good things helped me and made me a better person. Yet, there are bad things that we also learn that can ultimately hurt and even destroy us.

Satan's game plan is to use people to distract us and lead us down a road of doubt, uncertainty, hardship, and unbelief. Yes, this is real! Just look around sometime. Even good friends can lead you astray. I am certainly not saying not to make or have friends. We need relationships. Good relationships are necessary to make this world. God made us to be in fellowship with other human beings. I'm simply saying, don't just go along with others for the sake of getting along only to have relationships.

I remember my freshman year as a student at Florida State University. I joined a fraternity at the time mainly to have more friends. While I hated the pledge period that lasted twelve weeks, I really got to know and bond with the guys I was in line with, and some of them are still close friends today. These are what I call "healthy relationships." The opposite are those unhealthy relationships that are toxic and downright dangerous, causing you to be in a constant state of fear, sadness, anger, or depression. These relationships are life-threatening and you should run from them as fast as you can. Run like Forrest did in the movie *Forrest Gump*. I call this the *"RUN, FORREST, RUN!"* mode. When people around you are crazy or start to get crazy, run from them as fast as you can.

After I finished the pledge cycle and became a fraternity Greek, as they say, I found myself in a fraternity of guys with a wide range of personalities. Some were very strong and really different from any characters I had ever met at that time. And thank God for a great mom who raised me in a household with a strong belief system and where moral character was instilled in me. It helped and maybe even saved my life at times as, almost every weekend, I was pressured by some of my frat brothers to go out, smoke weed and get high, and just do things I knew were wrong. I was raised to believe that was not the right thing for me to do. So, I can honestly say I stayed away from most of the troubles and the wrong things. Was it me and my strength? No way! Without God, I would have caved to the temptations. I believe strongly even today that God was there for me, to help me in those situations, because He had a greater plan for my life.

Sure, there were other things I did in my life as a result of peer pressure that I am not proud of. Most of us can say that. The important question to answer is, who and what is influencing you? Do you know when you are being influenced in a bad way? Do you know that those wrong influences are designed to limit and even destroy your life? And, most important, do you know the source behind those bad influences?

The source or cause is the enemy, called the Devil or Satan. Do you know that even good intentions and even nice people like you can be deceived and led astray by Satan? Satan is a subtle, stealthy enemy who often speaks to you in your thought life using words that sound like your very own thoughts. Often, you think it is you saying and thinking these things.

For example, let's say your neighbor Jeff, who has been a friend of yours for many years, is out of town for a few days, and you know this because he asked you to watch his place for him while he is away. A voice in your mind says, *There are some very nice tools in Jeff's garage that you have always admired and wished you owned. Why don't you just take a few and make it look like a burglar broke in and took them?*

Why would you do that? Who is behind the voice telling you to steal Jeff's property? Would you actually do it? I certainly hope you would not. But this kind of voice talks to people all the time, and all too often otherwise good people and even Christians yield to it. Satan tries to convince you that the voice you are hearing is your own and that this idea of wrongdoing originated inside you.

Even when you tell yourself, "I cannot do that to Jeff. That would just be wrong," there comes another voice calling you a bad person. And if you are a Christian, the voice tells you that you must not be saved because Christians don't think that way. Yet voices like these originate with Satan or one of his demonic spirits. You need to expect this so that you will know what to do when they come, because they will come.

Speak to the Voices and Put Them Down

These voices that we are hearing in our head that are contrary to God's Holy Word (the Bible) come from Satan himself, demonic forces, and the pits of Hell. These voices manifest themselves in many different ways. They are clever and can sometimes hide themselves in the use of medically descriptive terminology, such as a panic disorder, hallucinations, bipolar disorder, and schizoaffective disorder. While I readily admit that I am not a medical doctor or expert, it is clear to see that these voices come from a dark place that not even medical science can fully understand or explain their origin. We must turn to the Word of God for additional clarity and understanding.

The Bible refers to these voices as "strongholds." Simply put, strongholds are thoughts and/or voices that Satan and/or his demons have put into the minds and thought lives of human beings to contradict everything good that God says and intends for mankind to have. The Word of God tells us and defines for us what strongholds are and how to deal with them. Here is what 2 Corinthians 10:3-5 (KJV) says.

> For though we walk in the flesh, we do not war after the flesh; For the weapons of our warfare are not carnal, but mighty through God to the pulling down of Strongholds; Casting down imaginations, and every high thing that exalted itself against the knowledge of God and bringing into captivity every thought to the obedience of Christ.

With these words and many more in the Bible, God has given to mankind the weapons we need to fight and defeat Satan's strongholds. These weapons include prayer, faith, hope, love, and the power and authority found in the Word of God. We see here, as an example, how the Word of God encourages us to stand strong against the Devil and his cohorts in Ephesians 6:13-17 (KJV). It says:

> Wherefore take unto you the whole armor of God, that ye be able to withstand in the evil day, and having done all, to stand. Stand therefore, having your loins girt about with truth and having on the breastplate of righteousness; and your feet shod with the preparation of the gospel of peace; above all, taking the shield of faith, wherewith ye shall be able to quench all the fiery darts of the wicked. And take the helmet of salvation, and the sword of the Spirit, which is the word of God.

It may seem unreal to you, but the Word of God is a mighty weapon that can and must be used against the enemy, Satan. Yes, this mighty weapon called God's Word can break down these Satanic voices you hear in your head. These words can break down the walls that Satan builds to keep you from believing in Jesus and all the great things He has done for mankind.

When the Bible says, in 2 Corinthians 10:5 (KJV), "Casting down imaginations, and every high thing that exalted itself against the knowledge of God, and bringing into captivity every thought to the obedience of Christ," what is it referring to or talking about? Simply put, here God is telling us that we, as human beings, have the authority to speak back to these voices when we hear them in our head.

Amazingly, God has given every Believer that authority. For example, a voice may be telling you that you have cancer and you are going to die. You know that your grandmother and your aunt both had this type of cancer and died from it, so you believe you will too. Many people will take that as the last word and give up and die. Giving up, giving in to your circumstances and quitting, is never the solution. Your immediate response should be to *speak faith*, speak the Word of God, to that sickness and disease enemy that has come against you. That includes speaking aloud to the Devil, "No you don't, Devil. You will not kill me with cancer or any other disease."

In 1 Peter 2:24 (KJV), the Bible says: "Who His own self bare our sins in His own body on the tree, that we, being dead to sins, should live unto righteousness: by whose stripes ye were healed." This means that Jesus has already paid the price for all of mankind by allowing himself to become a sacrifice for us on the cross. Jesus has paid the ransom, the great cost, for our sins so that we do not have to. This payment for us includes the payment for our healing. In God's eyes, the debt for mankind has been paid for our salvation and healing, if we accept and receive what Jesus has done for us. God wants us to heal and to be well and free from sickness and disease. That was God's original plan for mankind and still is. One of my favorite Bible verses, which I refer to all the time, is 3 John 2 (KJV): "Beloved, I wish above all things that thou mayest prosper and be in *health*, even as thy soul prospereth." This verse reminds me that God wants me healthy and well supplied with nothing missing or broken in my life.

Chapter Five

Alive for a Purpose

All of us, at some point in our life, ask ourselves the question: "What am I here for?" or "What is the purpose of my life?" For me, especially when I was younger, there was never a day that I did not think about my life's purpose.

As a young black male growing up in the 1960s and 1970s in a small town in the Deep South of the United States, I saw and experienced a life and times that were not always good. In fact, much of the time, life was harsh and challenging. Much of what I saw around me was racism and poverty. Like most African Americans in my generation and even my local community, my family endured regular financial shortages, hardship, and discrimination. Hard work to make ends meet was a part of our daily lives. After Dad died, Mom worked outside the house as a part-time housekeeper and, with ten children at home, she worked at home as a full-time housekeeper. These were just a few of the many difficult life conditions we experienced at that time.

I said to myself time and time again, "There has got to be more to life than what I see around me." I would watch my mother every day, a widow struggling to raise ten children on her own. I always knew that someway—someday and somehow—things had to be better than this. For so long I did not see a meaning or purpose to my life, yet I knew there had to be a better way.

Most of my local community at the time went to church, mostly on Sundays. Our small Baptist church was for us a place of refuge and fellowship. There we experienced an atmosphere of family and even a sense of importance. I will be eternally grateful for my early years of church and Sunday school experiences. It was there that I learned about God and our Savior Jesus Christ. These teachings helped me grow into the man I have become. As a young child and teenager, I received a general understanding of the Bible. The community, family, friends, and fellowship I got through my church experience helped me get through what would otherwise have been a sad, depressing, and difficult time in my life.

In my youth, the teaching and biblical understanding at my local home church was limited. I'm sure the preachers and the adults at the time taught me all they knew or understood. Unfortunately, it was just not enough for me. I was convinced at that time that there was more to know or understand. I simply did not know what understanding was or how to get it. It is difficult to find something when you don't know exactly what you are looking for. But I had to keep looking. There was always this voice on the inside telling me, "There is more to your life than you see right now." I needed to know who I was and what God's purpose for me was here on earth. No one around me seemed to have a good answer for me, so I had to keep looking.

I recall some years later having a few conversations about the "meaning of life" with my Sunday school teacher and my Boy Scout troop leader, who also happened to be my middle school teacher.

Teachers would almost always end the conversation with, "Just wait. You will find out the meaning of life as you grow up." There was some truth to that, but I didn't want to just wait until I grew up (like I had a choice). I wanted to know the answers now. But of course, that was not possible.

Meanwhile, I got questions from curious adults around me: "What do you want to be when you grow up?" and "What are your plans for your future after high school?" Never were there any explanations from the teachers or counselors to help answer the questions I had: "Who am I, this person choosing this career?" or "Why is it even necessary to choose a career?" By the time I graduated from high school, I wondered if anyone knew the answer to these questions. Like most of the young people I knew at the time, I just went through the motions of life. I did what I was told was best for me: Go to school! Get a good job! The best way to get a good job is to get a good education. While that was the direction my life went in, I always felt there was something missing.

After high school, I went to college and later went into the military as an active-duty U.S. Army officer. Years before that, during the Vietnam era, Gary had been drafted into the military, choosing to join the Marine Corps. Our military experiences just fueled each of our quests to know our true life purpose and understand why we were, each in our own way, having to experience the complicated challenges happening in our lives.

We each joined the military for much the same reasons: We were looking for a challenge, to further our education, and we had a strong desire for self-fulfillment. While we both were prepared to give our life in service to our country, we knew in our hearts that would not be our life's purpose. Even with the close calls with death that we both had in different places and at different times during war and combat, by the grace of God we each survived our time in the military and are still here.

The Danger of Self-Effort

There have been many books written and movies made about the purpose of life. I have read or watched many of them and none have ever fully satisfied me. Themes that many of these "life purpose" tools promote are *self-effort* and *self-reliance.* These advocate depending on oneself first, *before God*, for your survival and success in life. The ideas that self-effort and self-reliance promote are things like: "What do I think? What do I want? What is best for me? I know the answer, and the answer is …," and "I always know what's best for me, even when you don't know what is best for you."

Many people think that what they become in life depends exclusively on themselves and their own abilities. Many of us are taught this—to depend on ourselves first—from a very young age. I remember when I first learned to ride a bicycle. My older brother who taught me said, "I am only going to hold you up for a little while, then I am going to let you go. When I let you go, the rest is up to you and you have stay up on your own." Those words from my brother have stayed in my memory and promoted in me the principle of self-reliance. The world, we learn, which includes our loved ones, family, and friends, will help us only so far, and then the rest is up to us.

Yes, I did learn to ride the bicycle, but I missed an important lesson at the time—it's called trusting God and not just relying on my own abilities. Understanding God's intervention, protections, and grace is a process and not something you get all at once. I understand now that I did not just learn how to ride a bicycle; it was God Himself who gave me the ability and strength to ride the bicycle.

Now, it is critically important to understand the distinction here between *self-effort and self-reliance* versus *taking the initiative, being proactive, not being lazy, or just being unwilling to work.* The distinction is that, with self-effort and self-reliance, you are fully depending on your abilities, intellect, and education rather than on the wisdom that comes from Almighty God. This dependency on self often comes from a conscious or passive effort acquired over time from being in an environment or around people where you are literally indoctrinated in the "I will," "It's me," and "It's my way" mindset.

Where does this self-effort, self-reliance, "I will," and "It's my way" spirit come from? And yes, that is what it is—a spirit. It is called the spirit of "I will," and it comes from none other than Satan himself. Some may say, "Oh, there you go again blaming it all on the Devil." Satan or the Devil is rightly to blame because he is the source of all the evil on this earth. Is self-effort and self-reliance and the spirit of "I will" evil? Any time you put something or someone before God, including yourself, that attitude is motivated by an evil spirit originating with Satan. Making anything a higher priority than God does not please God. The Bible calls God a jealous God and nothing should come before Him (Exodus 20:5).

The Bible is very clear and tells us in the Book of Isaiah 14:12-17 that there is a spirit that is very anti-God and is very much alive and working to rule the world today. These verses describe Satan or the

Devil as Lucifer, which he was first called. Lucifer was the originator of this selfish spirit called "I will."

The Devil (Satan) has not always been an evil spirit. Satan once was an archangel residing in Heaven with Almighty God and the legion of other angelic beings (angels). Lucifer is described as a beautiful being full of gifts and talents. The very essence of Lucifer embraced and encompassed an anointed Heavenly sound. In Ezekiel 28:13-14 (KJV), God, speaking about Lucifer, said that He instilled in him a "workmanship of thy tabrets and of thy pipes" which was prepared in him on the day that he was created. God is referring to the great talents and gifts He gave Lucifer. The Bible also describes this being as a model of perfection, full of wisdom and beauty. However, this being became corrupted, and evil was found in him. God expelled him from Heaven. This being is, no doubt, Lucifer (Satan, the Devil). See Ezekiel 28:11-19 (KJV, AMPC, NIV); Luke 10:18 (KJV).

Yes, as we see later, evil was found in Lucifer. He became corrupted and rebelled against God. It is not clear how evil and jealousy got into Lucifer. This rebellion against God embodied the very essence of the selfish spirit of "I will." Lucifer wanted to be higher and greater than God. But, of course, he could not and can never be greater than the Almighty. Isaiah 14:12-17 (KJV) relates the fall of Lucifer. Note Lucifer's selfish thoughts of "I will" in verses 13 and 14.

12. How art thou fallen from Heaven. O Lucifer, son of the morning! How art thou cut down to the ground, which didst weaken the nation! 13. For thou hast said in thine heart, I will ascend into heaven. I will exalt my throne above the stars of God; I will sit also upon the mount of

the congregation, in the sides of the north: 14. I will ascend above the heights of the clouds, I will be like the Most High. 15. Yet thou shalt be brought down to hell, to the sides of the pit. 16. They that see thee shall narrowly look upon thee and consider thee, saying, is this the man that made the earth to tremble, that did shake Kingdoms; 17. That made the world as a wilderness, and destroyed the cities thereof; that opened not the house of his prisoners?

These verses of the Bible chronicle the raw and selfish ambition of Lucifer/Satan to not only be like God but also to be above Almighty God Himself. This selfish spirit is obvious and apparent in the many times the phrase "I will" is used. This selfish spirit of "I will" started with Lucifer and has existed ever since. Sadly, it still exists in the hearts of so many humans today.

These verses also show how, when this selfish spirit goes uncontrolled and unbridled, it can lead to destructive consequences in the world. Yet God shows us here that Satan is just a bully whose goal is to steal, kill, and destroy (John 10:10). But Satan and all who are on his side will ultimately be defeated. Don't be on Satan's side because your end too will be one of defeat and destruction. Finally, we note in Isaiah 14:15, that God reminds us that there is a Hell, it is real and that it is Satan's final place of defeat.

Is the Selfish Spirit Operating in You?

Is this selfish spirit operating in your life now? This selfish spirit causes your priorities to be about you and your needs first. It causes your first response to be about what you want, what is good for you, and what is in your best interests. That is selfish. God's priority is His Love and concern for all mankind. Likewise, we all, especially Believers, should be concerned with the welfare of others—of everyone.

As I've said, this selfishness is usually prompted or at least encouraged by the enemy, Satan. Satan wants your actions to not be good, kind, and generous, but rather to be self-serving and always contrary to the things of God. This selfish spirit is not just some unreal and made-up notion designed to confuse you. No, the selfish spirit is real. It is a human trait that exists and operates in every human to some degree from birth. Look at the example of a baby or toddler: They want what they want and will often cry loud enough and long enough until they get it.

We have all experienced being selfish sometime in our life. Rather than accept this as normal or just the way you are, the questions you must always ask yourself are: (1) "Do I recognize this selfishness?" (2) "Is it a regular part of my life?" (3) "Does it dominate my life and behavior as I relate to other people?"

The selfish spirit can be a subtle, innate, internal force operating in you without you even realizing it. It may manifest itself in a number of ways. For example, you may exhibit behaviors such as always wanting to be in control and in charge of a situation, program, or event. Things always have to go your way and you're not interested in the opinions of others.

I know this can be uncomfortable to talk about. Yet it is real and all too prevalent in our lives. Selfishness is internal, about oneself, and inconsistent with the God of Love, who cares about all of us. This selfish spirit is influenced by Satan himself and therefore cannot please God.

We all know someone like this friend of mine who I grew up with. He is a good person, and we were just teenage kids in high school together. Many times, when we would spend time together around other people, he seemed to always want to be the star of the show. He would go out of his way to try to impress people with what he knew, often at the expense of making me look bad or embarrassing me. His opinions and ideas always came first.

Then, one day, it all came to a head. I said to him in private, "Joe (I will call him Joe to protect his identity), we have been friends for a long time, and I gotta tell you, you don't always treat people well or with respect. What you do and say sometimes hurts and embarrasses me. You need to know that other people's opinions matter too. You need to change your behavior or we cannot be friends anymore." Yes, he was surprised that I would speak to him that way and even got a bit angry with me for a time. Later, he told me, "You were right. I have been thinking of myself mostly and not considering others." We made up and became friends again and still are today. My point here is that, after our conversation, Joe realized that his behavior was wrong. Fortunately, he was willing to change and not let a selfish spirit dominate his life.

All of us, at points in our life, consciously or unconsciously take on the spirit of selfishness or "I will," which manifests itself in many different ways. The Word of God tells us to walk in love with each other and to love our neighbors as we do ourselves (Matthew 19:19). Our lives cannot and should not always be about ourselves and what we want, but rather our hearts have to be open to the concerns and needs of others. That way, the Love of God and the Light of God can reflect and shine through us, and we can continue to be a glorious blessing to those around us.

It's Just Too Hard to Change

"What if I've discovered that I have this selfish spirit—how do I change my behavior? *Can* I change, or isn't it too hard or even impossible to change at my age?" you might be asking. There is not one of us who, at some point in our lives, hasn't seen something about ourselves that we would like to change. From the time I was a small boy, I have always wanted to be tall. At one point, I had hoped to be a professional basketball player. However, in examining my family history, I discovered that none of my male relatives were over six feet tall. Not my father, my brothers, nor any of my uncles. So how could I possibly be tall enough to one day play in the NBA? In the eleventh grade at high school, I was more than a reasonable height at 5'8" or 5'9", yet I wanted to be taller. Why, you might ask? I don't know, I just wanted to, or maybe because I was always told that girls really like tall men.

Everyone told me back then that it is impossible to be any taller than I was because by my age in the eleventh grade, the body has stopped growing. People told me, "You cannot control your height, and there is just not anything you can do about it." But no matter what they said, I decided I would ask God to be taller. I remember being alone in my bed at night just talking to God about being taller. No one knew about this but me and God. It wasn't important to anyone but me and God. I did this for months (maybe even years), asking God and believing, "I will be taller." Then time passed and I forgot about it.

But then one day during my sophomore year of college, I was having a conversation with friends and, to my surprise, one said to me, "You are tall." That's when it hit me, "You know, I *am* tall." To my amazement and that of those who knew me well, between the eleventh grade and my sophomore year in college, I had actually grown five inches. I went from 5'9" to my current height of 6'3". For years, I said I would be tall and believed it. Even though for a time I had just stopped thinking about being tall, the seeds had already been planted through my saying and believing it.

So, while I never became a great athlete or played college team sports, let alone became an NBA player, I did discover that *the impossible is sometimes very possible—if you believe*. I also learned that "With God, all things are possible" (Matthew 19:26 KJV). Why am I telling you this story, you might ask? Well, God cares about everything that concerns us, even those things that may seem small and trivial to us and others. God just loves us so much. "Saying it is important to having it." What you speak or confess, you can have. This is a biblical principle, called "You can have what you say," found in Mark 11:23.

Yes, there are things that are hard to change and things that seem impossible to change. There is one area in particular we all must work at every day to do better. That area is our behavior toward others. In other words, how you treat other people is vitally important. Treating others well not only positively affects the person you are kind to, but it also makes you feel better and you too become a better person. Changing your behavior and being a better person can be as simple as saying, "Lord, I want to change my behavior, but I need your help." Our God of Mercy will intervene to help you become the better person you want to be. The change you seek may not happen overnight, but if you ask God and believe, and if what you desire is in line and consistent with God's Word, it will happen for you.

It's Not about You

You are on the earth for a purpose. God created each of us and put us here for a purpose. This purpose is your *Divine destiny*, which is simply *God's plan for your life*. If you choose to believe and accept God's plan for your life, then your time on this earth will be a wonderful and gratifying experience.

You see, God has given each of us gifts and talents. According to 1 Corinthians 7:7, each man has his own gift from God. God knew what He was doing when He put specific gifts, talents, and strengths inside you. You may not realize you have a uniqueness or special gifts, but you do. Your gift may be singing, dancing, speaking, teaching, being an artist or a leader in business, working with your hands, or any number of other abilities God may have blessed you with. When you recognize your gift and begin to use it to help others, then God will further bless that gift, making it even better and stronger for you.

Your Divine destiny is simple to God, and God wants it to be simple for you. God's plan and purpose for you is for you to make a positive difference in the lives of other people. Your life on earth cannot be just about you or what is good for you only. It has to be about making a positive difference in the lives of others.

It is so easy to get caught up in the notion of "what is best for me," but that is not what God wants for you. God wants us to seek out our special gifts. You may already know what yours is, but if you don't, just ask God to reveal it to you. When you recognize your talent and begin using it for God's glory by making the lives of others better, it will bring you the greatest happiness and peace. Everyone asks, "What is my purpose?" The simple answer is, "To use your talents and gifts unselfishly to help others."

Gary's and my greatest inspiration for writing this book is to help and be a blessing to other people. For most of our lives, we have selfishly lived for what's good for us. When you live like that, a consequence is that your selfish behavior is ultimately harmful to you and others. As we look back on our lives, we see that people over the years have been adversely impacted by our selfish behavior. There is much we regret. Of course, there was much done that cannot be undone. And, there are some things we did and can still do to make things right. Where possible, it is always an important start to make amends to the person you hurt or impacted, ask God's forgiveness, and finally forgive yourself.

What we both have learned to do is repent and ask God for His mercy and forgiveness. We have seen through the years how God in His great grace and mercy has helped us and made things right. God has shown us that, "If we confess our sins, He is faithful and just to forgive us our sins and to cleanse us from all unrighteousness" (1 John 1:9 KJV). God also said, "All things work together for good to those who love God and who are called according to His purpose" (Romans 8:28 KJV).

You will see a change in your life when you step away from a life dictated by what's best for you toward a life concerned with how you can make a positive difference in the life of someone else. Please don't misunderstand, I am not saying I am perfect. Gary is certainty not saying he is perfect. We are saying that, with God through our Lord

Jesus Christ, our lives have changed for the better as we ask Him, Lord, to help us to focus less on self and focus on others to make this a better world. You can do the same thing too, if you choose.

Chapter Six

A Message to Our Grandchildren and the Next Generation

You are unique and special in God's eyes. Never make the mistake of undervaluing who you are.

If you have read the preceding chapters, I pray that you now understand these three things: (1) There is a God; (2) Life on this earth will end one day for each of us; and (3) There is a destination after earth for every human, which is Heaven or Hell. There is a Hell and it is real. The Hell that Gary experienced and told us about in Chapter One is a very real place. You don't want to go there. You have a choice whether to go to Hell. It is up to you.

Now there is a very special group of people we would like to focus on. This is the group I call the "next generation," which includes our children and grandchildren. While this is a special message for our family and young people, it is not just for them, but also for the new generation of Believers all over the world who are open to the truth. As you read this book, we trust you become a Believer of the truth of the Gospel through Jesus Christ. You have much to live for, and so many things will be vying for your attention. It is therefore vital that you seek the truth and recognize it when you see and hear it.

As a young kid, and even in your teen years, it is very easy to get lost in the notion, "I am still young and have my whole life in front of me. Why should I be concerned about the serious things in life right now?" You may think, *Just let the old folks worry about things like the rent, a mortgage, other bills, or retirement income one day. I just want to hang out with my friends and have some fun.* But there is one certainty in life: If you live long enough, you are going to get old too and when you do, you will wish you had learned a few more things when you were young that would have made your adult life a bit easier or better.

Sometimes, one of the best things you can do for yourself is to listen to someone who has more experience than you—that is, someone who has been around longer, seen and experienced more than you, and hopefully has wisdom they are willing to share with you. Between Gary and me, we have over 120 years of life experience and acquired wisdom. Some of the suggestions in this book come from very hard life experiences, from getting in fights and getting beat up, to going to jail, to nearly being killed in car accidents and military combat, and almost dying from COVID. These are all events in our lives that God got us through. We say, "Wow!" and "Praise God!" as it is only by His grace that we are still here to share this message with you now.

God has also given us the wisdom and patience to listen to others who are wiser than we are, as well as to do our own research and study. It is from these life experiences and personal study that we want to share with you some important life lessons that will hopefully help you avoid some of our more painful mistakes. This list entails some practical advice and simple tips that could one day literally save your life.

Some "Life Learned" and "Experience Taught" Lessons

Hello, children, grandchildren, next generation, other family, and friends. Here are eight very important "life learned" and "experience taught" lessons we want to share with you. We will list them first and then discuss them each in more detail. This is by far not an exhaustive list, but some necessary and vital points to live your life by.

1. **Everything that looks good is not necessarily good for you.**
2. **Choose your friends wisely.**
3. **Obey your parents and people in authority over you.**
4. **You may not be as smart as you think you are.**
5. **You will fall sometimes, but you do have the strength to get back up.**
6. **If you live long enough, you will get old too.**
7. **Choose the right side; stay on the right side.**
8. **Always trust God.**

1. Everything That Looks Good Is Not Necessarily Good for You

It is in the very nature of mankind to be attracted to what the eyes see that is pleasant and appealing to the senses. The allure of what you see that looks good is often hard to resist. Remember in the Garden of Eden, after God told Adam and Eve (meaning mankind) not to eat of the Tree of the Knowledge of Good and Evil, Eve was the first to be deceived by the enemy Satan in the disguise of a serpent. Satan convinced Eve that the fruit of the tree was good for her when it was not, as it had been forbidden by God. Eve found the fruit to be pleasant to her eyes and something to be desired, and so she ate it and then gave it to her husband, Adam, who was with her. (See Genesis 3:1-6.)

This is the very first event and the first example in the Bible where humans see something that looks good, is pleasant to the eyes, but certainly and ultimately is not good for them. This act of disobeying God was certainly not a good thing, as it had a tragic result not just for Adam and Eve, but for all of mankind. This single act of disobedience resulted in the spiritual death of mankind—mankind's spiritual separation from God. That one act of disobedience by mankind ended the Divine communion God shared with man in the Garden of Eden and allowed evil to come into the world and become a dominant force on earth. While God still loves mankind, it was mankind alone who created a separation between him and God that could only be cured by accepting a relationship with Jesus Christ as Lord and Savior.

As you can see from this epic example, it is very easy to get lured into wanting to have things that look good. Our human nature, lust, and zeal for the beautiful and attractive things in life often pull us in that direction. Satan is the enemy to mankind, and that enemy often exploits our desires and cravings for good things. It is not necessarily a bad or wrong thing to desire the good things in life, because, after all, God gave us that human trait. What makes desires for certain things wrong or inappropriate depends on our motives.

Motives are the "why" behind what we do. Why do you want what you want? Is it for selfish reasons? Do you just want to keep up with the other guy? Do you crave or are you jealous of what someone else has?

Family and friends, the best advice I can give you about motives is to keep them honest. An honest motive is being inspired to help others and to be a blessing to others in your zeal to have good and beautiful things. Always ask yourself the question, "How is what I am desiring a help or blessing to someone else?" You will be amazed at how your thoughts to help others first can quickly turn into a blessing for you as well.

Again, Gary and I readily admit that our lives are far from perfect and, for much of them, we have not been focused on what benefits others. Most of our lives have been spent seeking things that only pleased ourselves, without even a second thought of how others may be helped. And, if you are being honest with yourself, you will see that your life is probably that way too. That's because that is our nature as human beings.

For much of my life, if I saw something and it was nice or looked good, I wanted it, and usually right away. I remember even as a seven-year-old boy wanting a particular beautiful, shiny ten-speed bicycle. "What could possibly be wrong with a seven-year-old boy wanting a ten-speed bicycle?" you might ask. Probably nothing. There is nothing wrong with the desire; it was my motive and the timing that were the issue. I was thinking only of me with this desire and not about the overall good or needs of my family.

All I knew was that the bicycle looked good in the store window every time I walked by, and I certainly desired it. It never occurred to me at the time that my family simply could not afford it. Of course, my mother was a very direct person and she told me straight out, "Son, we just cannot afford to get you a ten-speed bicycle when I have ten other mouths to feed." To my mom, putting food on the table for her family was much more important than a bicycle. For her, it was not a choice—it was a no-brainer.

After having a long talk with my mom, I realized that what I wanted may not be what I should have at that moment. The timing of getting what you want matters greatly. What also matters is how getting what you want will impact the lives of other people. Mom showed me how getting the bicycle could cause hardship for the family at that time. Despite my mom's strong desire to see me happy by getting a new bike, she recognized the wisdom and necessity of prioritizing the well-being of our entire family over the personal gratification of just one of her children.

Another valuable lesson arose from my longing for this bicycle when I, with the help of my brothers and friends, learned how to build my own bicycle. My brothers, cousins, friends, and I would scour old junkyards in search of discarded or abandoned bicycle parts. We would scavenge through our neighbors' garbage, explore local stores' discarded items, and delve into backyards, all in search of unused and abandoned items. Our relentless quest continued until we had collected enough functional parts to assemble our very own bicycles.

These were fun times spent hanging out with friends and family, and they brought my brothers, friends, and me closer together. While the bikes we made were not new and shiny, they were efficient and got us to our destinations with only occasional breakdowns. The wonderful thing about making your own bike is the pride of seeing and saying, "Wow, here is something I created." Most important, it helped me to overcome this constant desire for something beautiful and new.

2. Choose Your Friends Wisely

As young boys, we hung out a lot with kids our age. It's interesting how when you're young, it doesn't matter so much who you are hanging out with. The main goal is to have fun and seek relationships. It is true that all of us desire to be liked by others, and I get the importance of having friends. However, I hope that eventually you reach a point in your life where you recognize that it matters who you spend your time with.

This really deserves to be said loud and with special emphasis, "Who you spend your time with matters … a lot." It matters to your happiness. It matters to your success. It matters to your health and well-being. In fact, it plays a large role in determining your whole future. And, last but not least, it matters to God. Be careful who you call your friend. Friendship requires caring, concern, responsibility, accountability, and much more. Never take the word "friend" lightly.

I was deeply impressed by a passage in the Book of Proverbs that emphasizes the significance of friendship. This Scripture really helped me grasp the essence of a true friend and understand the distinction between a worldly friend and a godly friend who genuinely loves and cares for our relationship. This verse reads: "The man of many friends [a friend of all the world] will prove himself a bad friend, but there is a friend who sticks closer than a brother" (Proverbs 18:24 AMPC).

You may have many friends in this world, also known as worldly acquaintances. However, they are not truly friends in the real sense. Often, they have hidden motives and reasons for being in a relationship with you—selfish motives and the intent to get something from you, like money, promotion, power, a better position, or to improve their own status.

On the other hand, a godly friend is a genuine person who genuinely cares about you. They understand the value of a godly relationship and are willing to put in the effort to nurture and strengthen it. Usually, this person has a personal relationship with Jesus. The Bible refers to them as a true friend, one who sticks closer than a brother.

You may have various motives for wanting to be friends with other people. However, it is important to acknowledge that sometimes those motives may lack honesty and genuineness. What is your reason for seeking relationships and friendships at this point in your life? Is it to be a blessing to someone you genuinely care about, or is it solely for personal gain that benefits only you?

As I mentioned before, people pursue relationships for all kinds of reasons. You need to be honest with yourself about your intentions. Do you have what it takes to be a godly friend? There are times when people feel lonely and are in need of love and companionship. They may be very vulnerable and in need of someone who genuinely cares. Your willingness to be there for them could potentially save their life.

But if your motives for pursuing a friendship are not pure, it can greatly devastate that person, potentially causing lasting harm. Are you the kind of person who can get your mind off your own needs and readily help others in their moments of need? What kind of friend are you?

I remember hearing a story from a friend I'll call Jeff. Jeff had another male friend who he had known for many years, who I will refer to as Tim.

Jeff and Tim had what you might call a friends/buddies relationship. They would often hang out together, watching NFL football on Sundays with other guys, occasionally playing cards or bowling. Jeff viewed their relationship as just hanging out together and having fun. Their conversations were usually centered on topics like music collections, and they would often engage in lighthearted banter and jokes, never getting into anything too serious.

Then, unexpectedly, Tim's wife of many years passed away, leaving him devastated. It was in this moment that Jeff realized that Tim really needed a friend to talk to and support him through this difficult time. Jeff was willing to step up and be more than just a fun buddy to Tim. He recognized the importance of being available to Tim, providing the emotional and spiritual support that only a godly friend could offer during such challenging circumstances. Thank God Jeff had this awareness and could make the necessary adjustment in their relationship. It was truly a time when Tim needed a godly friend.

Like Tim, we all need a godly friend in our desperate times of need. It is vital that we ask God to show us and to lead us to godly friends and relationships. Equally important is developing the character of a godly friend through prayer and the study of the Word of God (the Bible). Remember, the world is full of "friend wannabes," but a true godly friend is one who sticks closer than a brother.

3. Obey Your Parents and People in Authority over You

"Children, obey your parents in the Lord: for this is
right. Honor thy father and mother; which is the first
commandment with promise; That it may be well
with you, and that you may live long on the earth."
—*Ephesians 6:1-3 (KJV)*

"Children, obey your parents in all things:
for this is well pleasing unto the Lord."
—*Colossians 3:20 (KJV)*

"I exhort therefore, that, first of all, supplications,
prayers, intercessions, and giving of thanks, be
made for all men; For kings, and for all that are in
authority that we may lead a quiet and peaceable
life in all godliness and honesty. For this is good
and acceptable in the sight of God our Savior."
—*1 Timothy 2:1-3 (KJV)*

So, what does it mean to obey your parents and people in
authority over you? Why is this kind of obedience so important?
Are these just fancy words, or do they have deeper meaning? Well,
they are indeed special words, but most important, they are words
and commands inspired by God. These commands are given to all
of us so that we can have a more peaceable and successful life on this
earth. God knew it was vital for children to respect and obey their
parents, which is why He made it the first commandment with a
promise. The promise God made to children who obey their parents
is that they will have a long life on this earth.

What does obeying your parents mean? It simply means listening to your parents, respecting them, and recognizing that their life experience and level of maturity are greater than that of the child. As a son or a daughter, it is important to acknowledge that their role as parents gives them a higher position, a ranking bestowed on them by God Himself. Along with this position comes authority over you, but also the responsibility to nurture you into a responsible and godly adult.

I am not saying that parents are perfect. None of us are. Parents don't know everything, and they certainly make mistakes too. We all make mistakes. Remember, God established a system of order, and He wants mankind to adhere to that order. When you respect your parents and people in positions of authority (such as political authorities, elected and appointed officials, teachers, police officers, school officials, and others), you are also showing respect to God. Yes, it begins with respecting your parents as a child. When you learn to respect your parents, it becomes easier to respect other authorities.

I remember the story of a seven-year-old boy. This little boy would have severe dreams and nightmares several times a week, which led to a fear of the dark and of dying. He was afraid that he would not live past his twelfth birthday. One Sunday, while attending Sunday school, the teacher taught a lesson from Ephesian 6:1-3 on how a child should obey his parents. The little boy thought, *Well, I do obey my parents.* However, he was still unsure if he was obeying them well enough. That night, he knelt down and prayed to God, asking for help to better obey his parents. The boy said, "Lord, I don't want to die by the age of twelve." After the prayer, the little boy decided to take God at His Word, and he committed to obeying his parents. Of course, there were times when he made mistakes or forgot his promise to obey. In those moments, he would quickly repent and ask his parents and God for forgiveness. That young boy has now reached sixty years old and is doing well and going strong. That young boy is me.

No doubt, we are currently living in difficult and perilous times. There is societal unrest and division among groups of people. These times bring with them an increasing disregard for authority. It is too easy to be swayed by the rest of the world and join the crowds in promoting disorder and disrespect for authority. Many of our cities have chosen to reallocate funds and resources away from their police departments, resulting in a reduction in the number of police officers and an increase in crime rates. When we fail to respect and appreciate our authorities, we will face dire consequences and ultimately witness a collapse in our society. Trust in God by obeying His laws and show obedience to those in positions of authority.

4. You May Not Be as Smart as You Think You Are

It is very easy to fall into the trap of thinking you know it all. Do you know anyone like that? Is that you? Believe me, there is not one person who knows it all and has all the answers. That is not how God created us. If we knew it all and had all the answers, we wouldn't need God.

Of course, we don't have all the answers, and we most certainly need God. You see, that is the very point. Many people think they know and have all the answers, so they don't think they need God. They believe God is irrelevant and unimportant. It's a big mistake to think that way, and a dangerous trap to put yourself in.

Just take a moment to look around. We live on an amazing planet in an incredible world. There are plants, water, air, and countless creatures and creations, including us humans. Surely, none of us could have made all of this; only God could. Only a God of Love, a Heavenly Father, could have accomplished such greatness and magnificence.

It is so important that we take the time to look around, recognize, and admit that there is Someone greater than we are. That will be the point that you can start to see that maybe, just maybe, you are not as smart as you think you are. When we bring ourselves back to this place, to a point of humility and openness to God's direction, that is when God can use us for His greater glory.

One of my favorite Scriptures in the Bible, which resonates deeply with me and has become a part of my life, is Proverbs 3:5-6 (NIV). It reads: "Trust in the Lord with all your heart and lean not on your own understanding; in all your ways acknowledge Him, and He will make your paths straight." These are more than words—they are wisdom and guidance spoken by God that have inspired and changed my life. I read or think on these words almost every day. Just the other morning when I woke up, I had an awareness unlike any I have had before. It was one of those times in life when it seemed like everything was going wrong. We all have experienced days like this. There was so much pressure from credit card bills, job stress, relationships, and responsibilities. I felt overwhelmed and did not know what to do.

The answer for me was to ask for help. No, not human help, as I did not know anyone around who could assist me in such a complex state of being. I had to turn to the one who I *knew* had the answer: my Father, God in Heaven.

I found a quiet place at home away from everything and everyone, and I simply had a conversation with God. I said to Him, "God, I have so much stress and pressure on me right now, and I really need Your help. I don't know what to do. I am not smart enough in my own ability or strength to figure it out." As I have learned from so many times in the past, God always hears me and answers my pleas for help.

Here's how I do this: First, as I go to God, I thank Him for listening to me, hearing me, and caring about me with His Love. Expressing gratitude to God first, and giving Him the glory and praise, has the effect of calming me down and making me feel more at ease.

Second, God then begins to show me the way. He sometimes puts people in my path to help me and give me words of wisdom and advice. God often shows me favor that I do not deserve and have not earned. What's also amazing is God gives me wisdom to know what to say in a situation where, in my natural abilities, I don't have the knowledge or skill to handle.

Let me give you an example. I am the presiding officer of a volunteer organization that I run. During one of our meetings that I was leading, an important question was asked by one of our members. No one knew the answer. Everyone in the room looked at me, expecting me to know. But I didn't know the answer either, at least not in my natural ability. As they all waited for me to respond, I quietly and in my spirit said to God, "Lord, what would you have me say?"

Before I knew it, these amazing words of wisdom began to flow from my mouth. The entire room of people looked at me with astonishment. Even I was surprised at how good God is. I give Him the glory for giving me the right words to say at the right time. This has not just happened once, but time and time again. I have learned to trust and rely on God.

You may be thinking, *Well, this just sounds strange or even weird. Things like that don't just happen.* Yet, I can assure you that it did. God is real, and He supernaturally works in our lives. He can work miracles in your life too, if you just let Him.

It starts with humility. Just humble yourself before the Lord and say, "Lord, I don't know everything, and I don't know what to do, but I know You do. Lord, I need Your help now. Give me the wisdom I need for this situation." When you have even that simple conversation with God, He hears you and answers your request. God gives us wisdom, and all we have to do is ask Him for it (James 1:5 KJV).

God created you and me, and He knows everything about us. God takes pleasure in helping us when we call on Him in the name of His Son, Jesus. Doesn't it make sense to let Him help you in your times of need? Just remember, while God gives us wisdom when we ask Him, we (mankind) are not the Source or Creator of that wisdom. God is. So, no, you are not as smart as you think you are!

> "If any of you is deficient in wisdom, let him
> ask of the giving God [Who gives] to everyone
> liberally and ungrudgingly, without reproaching
> or faultfinding, and it will be given him."
> —*James 1:5 (AMPC)*

5. You Will Fall Sometimes, But You Do Have the Strength to Get Back Up

You have lived long enough by now to know that everything in life will not go well for you all the time. You may experience debt and financial problems; there may be accidents, injuries, sickness, or disease around you. You will face the death of loved ones. Not everyone will always like you or want to be your friend. You will encounter anger, sadness, heartache, pain, and disagreements with others. These are just some of the many experiences you will have on this earth.

Yet, as human beings, it is in our nature to dream of and long for a perfect life and to dislike it when bad things happen. At some point in our lives, we all ask ourselves if there is such a thing as a perfect place where these bad things don't occur. Yes, there is such a perfect life and place. That place is called Heaven. If you accept Jesus as your Lord and Savior, you will experience the joy of Heaven when you leave this earth.

However, it's important to remember that we live in a reality on earth that is also inhabited by Satanic forces whose mission is to steal, kill, and destroy mankind (John 10:10). As long as we reside on this earth, we will experience both good times and trials and challenges. Jesus Himself tells us in the Gospel of St. John that there will be tribulations for mankind on this earth.

In John 16:33 (KJV), Jesus said, "These things I have spoken unto you, that in me ye might have peace. In the world ye shall have tribulation; but be of good cheer; I have overcome the world." There is joy and comfort in knowing that Jesus has overcome the world, depriving it of power to harm you, and has conquered it for you.

I want to encourage you with the realization that no matter what happens in your life, even if it is something bad that tries to bring you down, with Jesus, you have the ability to get up again. Hard and difficult times are part of life. At this point in your life, you may still be young and have not yet experienced the tough times that will inevitably come. But remember, you are more prepared than you think for those tough times.

God has placed within you the ability to rise up. If you were not capable of overcoming, God would have never allowed you to face the challenges that lie ahead. God tells us that when we have done all we can to stand, to stand therefore (Ephesians 6:13-14). This means that in times of adversity, we have the ability to keep going and keep standing. It also means that if you fall, you have the strength to get back up and keep standing.

This ability to get up and keep standing is called persistence and not quitting. There have been so many times in my life where I wanted to give up and quit.

Being a young black male growing up in a southern rural United States town, in a family living at or below the poverty level, there were not many opportunities for encouragement or optimism. Yet, I had to keep going. I knew I needed help, so I always looked for positive examples or good role models. Believe me, if you look around hard enough and long enough, you will find people out there who are willing to help you. God will somehow put those kinds of people in your path.

I found help and encouragement along the way, sometimes in the most unlikely places. I got help from teachers, coaches, aunts, uncles, cousins, and, of course, my dear mother. Although circumstances will certainly try, never let this life stop you or get you down. Know that God loves you and will never leave you or forsake you (Hebrews 13:5). You will fall sometimes, but you do have the strength to get back up.

6. If You Live Long Enough, You Will Get Old Too

Most of us don't like to think about getting old. Perhaps it's because getting older can be seen as boring, depressing, or even frightening, making us contemplate death or dying. On the other hand, being young and vibrant is exciting. At various points in our lives, we dream of always having that youthful life and being full of energy. However, the reality for all of us is that if we live long enough, we will inevitably grow older.

When I was a little kid, about six or seven years old, I could not wait to grow older and become an adult. I believed being an adult meant I could drive, own my own car, have a job, and earn my own money. I thought adulthood would be the perfect life I had always dreamed of.

As a child, that's how I saw it. But now that I am an adult, the realities of adulthood have set in, and things don't always seem as perfect as I had imagined. Being an adult comes with many obligations and responsibilities. While adulthood certainly has its advantages, the nonstop glamour and excitement I dreamed there would be often take a backseat to the daily toil of going to work and paying the bills.

The reality is, as we get older, things inevitably change. We must adapt and adjust to survive in this world because we are no longer children. To my fellow adults out there, I see you smiling in agreement. I believe you have discovered this truth as well.

Now, have you ever asked yourself why we, as mankind, were created to go through this growth and maturity process? Why didn't God just create us as full-grown adults from the beginning? Why do we have to go through stages of being babies, youths, teens, and then adults?

In the Bible, God is referred to as "Love" and "Wisdom." He is the All-Wise God. As our Creator, God knew it was important to mankind's spiritual maturity that our growth be a process and one that takes time. Mankind's growth process is not just physical, but mental and spiritual.

One of the greatest and most amazing gifts bestowed on us by God is the gift of time. It is also referred to as God's patience and God's long-suffering. What this means is that God, in His Divine benevolence, has given us time to get things right with Him.

As we discussed in an earlier chapter, God has granted mankind *free will,* which is the ability to make our own choices. Well, sometimes when we make our own choices, we get it wrong. God's patience and long-suffering provide us, as human beings, with the opportunity to realize our mistakes, repent from them, seek forgiveness, and redirect our lives according to God's will. God is often referred to as the God of Second Chances. Why does He offer us these second chances? Is it because He has to? No, it is because He wants to, because He loves us.

Growing up entails the process of physical and mental growth and maturity. Our spiritual growth and maturity, on the other hand, comes from the time we spend with God in prayer and studying His Word. This process is often referred to as renewing our minds, as mentioned in Romans 12:2. Renewing our minds spiritually does not occur overnight but is a lifelong journey of connecting with God through our time spent with Him. We should desire to know God and thank Him every day for His patience in letting us get to know Him.

We so often want to do things our way and to live our lives in a selfish and misguided fashion. We are frequently misguided by worldly influences rather than following what God would have us do. For instance, God may want you to use the incredible singing talent He has given you to share and spread His Gospel (Good News), but instead, you choose to use your gift to become a rock-n-roll singer. Don't misunderstand me—I'm not saying that singing rock and roll is inherently wrong. But if that is not what God has called you to do with your gift, then your gift is being misplaced.

God's patience allows us the opportunity to "get things right," to "correct our ways," according to His will for us. God can be very patient with us sometimes, waiting on us a long time to get things right with Him. But sometimes, He may not wait a long time. Unfortunately, we never know how long we have to get things right with God. That is why it is so important for us to treat each day as special and live as if it could be our last day on earth, because it may very well be.

Growing old is a privilege and gift from God. Not only is it a time to get things right, but it is also a time to help others get things right with God. This is one of the reasons why we are writing this book. God has called us to help others understand the importance of getting things right with God before it is too late.

One of the realities of life on this earth is, unless Jesus comes first (in the Rapture), we will all eventually die and leave this planet. We should again be thankful for the privilege of living long enough to discover and accept Jesus as our Lord and Savior. However, we must also remember that God knows the ultimate and greatest reality is life after death. God's patience grants us the time to choose life with Him in Heaven.

In various ways, God also reveals to us the alternative to life, which is eternal death in Hell. As we have shown you, Hell is a real place worse than any imaginable horror. Nothing you have ever heard of, read about, or seen in a horror movie can come close to the realities of Hell. The choice not to go there is yours to make.

As you live and grow older, rejoice in the gift of life, but most important, receive the greatest gift of all—life in Christ Jesus.

7. Choose the Right Side; Stay on the Right Side

Choosing the right side is crucial for obtaining eternal life. Staying on the right side is imperative for experiencing peace and serenity in our earthly lives.

I will remind you that God gave mankind a clear choice as to what side to choose, and He reminds us which side is the right side. In Deuteronomy 30:19 (AMPC), God says, "I call heaven and earth to witness this day against you that I have set before you life and death, blessings and cursing; therefore choose life, that you and your descendants may live."

God in His word is telling us we have a choice in this life. The right side is *life* and the wrong side is *death*. God, in His grace and mercy, even gives us a hint, just in case we are not smart enough to figure it out for ourselves. He tells us to "choose life."

Many people live their lives based on intellectual or mental decisions, rather than by heart decisions inspired by God. They may say, "I will do the right thing and try to live right." They convince themselves that they are good people and, for the most part, treat others well. However, a decision to do right made solely by the mind is temporary and can easily change depending on the circumstances of life. On the other hand, a decision made in the heart is influenced and guided by the Holy Spirit and even by God Himself. Remember, this heart I am referring to here is not your physical heart, but your human spirit on the inside of you that is being guided and directed by the Holy Spirit.

While it is important to be a good person and treat people right, *being good without God is not enough to save you from eternal death.* Only Jesus can provide salvation. Only through a relationship with Jesus can you be saved. And only with a relationship with Jesus are you able to make a decision from the heart.

I remember about ten years ago, I attended a meeting where an older gentlemen, age 103 at that time, was a special guest. He was in remarkable shape for his age. Accompanied by his grandson, he stood on his own without any assistance. His skin appeared healthy, and he was well-dressed. He stood tall and straight like a man with direction and purpose. When he spoke, his voice was clear and easily understood. The leader of the meeting then asked him to share a few words with the audience. Naturally, everyone was curious about how he had managed to live so long and be so well at such an advanced age.

This gentleman's words to the audience were simple and direct. He said, "You all must be wondering how I have lived so long." He said, "First, I thank God every day and give Him the glory." Then he said, "Stay on the right side. I attribute my longevity to staying on the right side, which is God's side."

I will never forget those plain but profoundly inspiring words. Having lived for over a century, this man had clearly faced and overcome many challenges in his life. At that moment, he stood before us as a living testament of his ability to conquer life's trials. His joy came from living on the right side and then being able to tell us that the secret to his longevity and well-being was staying on the right side, God's side. Clearly, he has enjoyed a peace on earth and one day is looking forward to an eternal peace with God, the Father, in Heaven. He lived well beyond the age of 103, a remarkable achievement and a reflection of his unwavering faith.

Please remember that even after you make the decision to accept Jesus as your Lord, there will be relentless forces trying to pull you back to the other side. Satan does not want you to be free from his control. One of Satan's greatest deceptions is making you believe that you are in control with the wrong thoughts that he, Satan, has suggested to you. Satan will have you believe that these wrong thoughts are from you and not him. The reality is that Satan is, all the while, attempting to manipulate you with his wrong thoughts. Remember, Satan is a liar and the father of all lies (John 8:44). But God does not and cannot lie. (See Titus 1:2.)

The biggest lie Satan tells mankind is that you don't have to believe in God. Satan is cunning, crafty, and subtle in his attempts to convince you that you know better than God, that God's Word is not true, that God does not keep His promises or care about you, or even that God does not exist at all. This is Satan's strategy. At some point in our lives, we have all heard these kinds of thoughts and voices in our heads. They are always Satan's lies and deceptions. Don't be deceived and taken in by these lies. If you fall for these deceptions, you are on the wrong side.

God is truly great and incapable of lying. In His Word, the Bible, God has provided many gifts and promises to mankind. Throughout this book, I have cited many passages from the Bible to support these truths. Ultimately, it comes down to whether you choose to believe them. Our goal is not to force you to believe that there is a God, a Satan, or even a Hell. We can't do that. Our purpose here is simply to give you a reason to believe that these things are real based on God's Word, the Bible, and our own personal life experiences. Even God Himself cannot make you believe. Though He wants you to believe, He respects your freedom to choose.

So, ask yourself this important question: Why would you want to serve a god that forces you to believe him? Such a god would not be the God of Love, but a god of evil (Satan).

8. Always Trust God

Are you still reading this book, and have you figured it out yet? Hell is a real place. Hell is eternal damnation and death with no way out and you want to and must stay out of it. But it is your choice. You have everything to say about the decision of whether you go to Hell. As important as avoiding Hell is, many people just don't want to hear anything about it. They don't want to hear any preachers; they don't want to read the Bible. "Oh, it just depresses me to hear all that stuff," some say.

I get it. Most people don't want to think about it. I am around people all the time who think talking about Hell is unpleasant, and the whole subject puts them in fear. Believe me, as unpleasant as talking about it may feel now, nothing compares to experiencing this place of doom, from which you cannot get out. God is our Heavenly Father, and He loves us so much that He has sent some people like Gary and me to share with you the experience of Hell. But most important, He sent a Savior named Jesus to keep us all out of Hell, if only we will believe in Him.

"But," you might be asking, "what about my life on this earth now—because sometimes I feel like I am in a kind of Hell." The same God of Love who wants to keep you out of Hell wants you to have a great life while you are on this earth. Some people believe that it is impossible to live a good life on this earth serving God. Some people believe our life on this earth will be too confined and controlled if they trust God. Some say, "Well, the Bible has too many restrictions. I would not be able to do what I want because I would always have to comply with all of God's many rules. I just want my freedom."

I have heard all the reasons and have even come up with some myself. Yet you must know that God created fun and He wants us to have a good time on the earth too. Yes, He really does. Why do you think God gave us emotions, joy, and the ability to laugh and to love? He gave us the ability to experience these things because He wants us to enjoy this life on earth. God just wants us to enjoy this life in the context of what is right and holy, of what is respectful and not harmful to ourselves or our fellow human beings. We do get to enjoy life on this earth, which means being happy and at peace, all in the context of trusting God and obeying His law and precepts.

I remember a story I once heard about a little girl named Jennie. She was only about four years old. She really loved her dad, and you might say she was a daddy's girl. Like many little kids her age, she experienced a lot of fears and uncertainties. There was the fear of heights, the fear of the dark, and the fear of large bodies of water. In an effort to help her overcome her fears, her father thought he would teach her to swim. That was proving to be difficult because Jennie was afraid to get into the pool. The father decided to step into the pool alone while Jennie stood on the edge. As he stood in the pool with his arms wide open, he told her, "Jennie, jump into my arms and I will catch you. I will not let you fall." He said, "Jennie, I love you. Do you trust me?" She said, "Yes, I trust you, Daddy." Jennie then jumped into the pool into her dad's big protective arms and they held each other tightly. Jennie said, "Daddy, I love you," and he replied, "I love you too." That is exactly how our God wants us to trust Him. We are to leave our troubles behind, on the edge where they are, and jump into God's Trusting and Loving arms, knowing that He is there to catch us and comfort us.

Will your life then suddenly be picture perfect? Will you never have any problems when you trust God? I am not saying that you will never have any problems; you will. Jesus Himself tells us that we will have troubles: "These things, I have spoken unto you, that in me ye might have peace. In the world ye shall have tribulations; but be of good cheer, I have overcome the world" (John 16:33 KJV). Tribulations simply means trials, trouble, difficulties, and hard times. The comfort we enjoy as Believers is knowing that, whatever challenges come our way, our Lord Jesus is there for us to help us overcome them. Jesus has already conquered the world for us, so we don't have to.

What I am saying to you, family and friends, is that with God through our Lord Jesus, you can overcome any problem. It is therefore essential that we trust God!

Chapter Seven

Why Was I Born, and Why Did Jesus Die for Me?

"Why was I born?" This is an age-old question and one that, no doubt, has been asked by countless past generations and will be asked by countless more to come. There has been so much guessing and speculation, so many theories and commentaries, about why God let us be born and what His plan is for our lives. Answers to these and similar questions have come from people all over the world over time, and many of these people are perhaps much smarter and wiser than I am. I don't presume to know all of the answers, and I am not about to give you some list of things I made up. But what I do know is that God has made available to all of us a book called the Bible, which is His written Word full of wisdom, understanding, and revelation. In my lifetime, I have grown to understand that God's written Word, the Bible, should be the very core and foundation of our existence. It certainly has become my source for discovering who I am and why I am here. I believe that God desires the Bible to serve as the direction and guide for all people.

What is the Bible, and why was it written? The answers to these questions are summarized in two Scripture verses found in the Bible, in 2 Timothy 3:16-17 (AMPC).

16. Every Scripture is God breathed (given by His inspiration) and profitable for instruction, for reproof and conviction of sin, for correction of error and discipline in obedience, and for training in righteousness (in holy living, in conformity to God's will in thought, purpose, and action). 17. So that the man of God may be complete and proficient, well fitted and thoroughly equipped for every good work.

If you are not familiar with the unique wording of the Bible, it may be difficult to understand at first. It was for me. So I kept asking God to help me better understand His Word and to surround me with godly people who could teach and explain His Word to me correctly and with clarity.

In 2 Timothy 3:16-17, it tells us that He inspired men to write the Bible, and that the Bible was inspired and given to men by God because God knew what we humans needed to survive and prosper in this world and to make it to the Divine world that is yet to come. God says His Word is to instruct by giving us understanding of how and where to go in life. The Word convicts us by revealing what is wrongful and sinful, and it corrects us to prevent us from committing these sins. The Word trains us on how to become righteous through a relationship with Jesus Christ and teaches us how to live a righteous life. Finally, in verse 17, God desires for us to live a complete and fulfilled life, equipped and prepared to do the good works He has planned for us. No matter what your job or chosen profession may be, God wants to be involved in helping you and making your life better.

Does God Need Us to Be God?

The Bible tells us in the first chapter of Genesis that God is the great Creator. "In the beginning, God created the heaven and earth" (Genesis 1:1-21 KJV). Everything good that we know, see, and experience comes from God (James 1:17). God is the Source and Creator of the Universe. He looked upon His creation and called it good.

God also created humanity in His image and likeness (Genesis 1:26-27). You may wonder who created God and how He came into existence. God calls Himself the Alpha and Omega, the First and the Last, the Beginning and the End (Revelation 1:11). This suggests that God has no beginning and will never have an end. He has always existed and He will never cease to exist or perish.

I know that, for some, this is hard to fathom and understand, but for Believers of faith, we acknowledge the existence of such a God and affirm it within the depths of our being.

So then, why did this all-powerful and all-knowing God, who created the Universe and all life itself, choose to create humanity? Did God need man in order to be who He is? No, certainly not. But we do need God in order to be who we are.

God created mankind because God is Love. He's more than just the God of Love, He is Love itself (1 John 4:8). God is the very definition of Love. So, as the God of Love, it was natural for God to want to share that love with beings like Himself. This is why God created man in His own image and likeness.

Similar to God, human beings are spiritual beings with a soul. While God had also created plant life and various forms of animal life, fellowship with these creations was not possible because they did not belong to the same spiritual class as God. God cannot have a deep connection with an elephant or a mountain lion, as they are not of the same spiritual class. That is, other animals were not made in the image and likeness of God. They were never meant to be God's heirs, sons and daughters, like mankind was intended to be.

Simply put, God created mankind because the great God of Love desired to have a family. As spiritual beings, made in God's image, we humans are an integral part of God's family. We have been chosen to enter into a relationship with Him, to experience His love, and to reflect His character in the world.

It is important to understand that the God of Love, who created us to be a part of His family, respects our freedom of choice, which includes whether to be a part of His family. As much as God wants us to be a part of His family, He will never impose Himself on us or force us to love Him or to join His family.

God grants us the gift of free will mentioned in a previous chapter. Consider this: Can you ever imagine forcing someone to be your friend? While you may be able to bribe or pay someone to act as your companion for a little while, is that a real or genuine friendship? You know the answer to that question.

So, with all that is happening in this world now—sin, evil, hatred, distrust all around us—some wonder: Did God change His mind about being our friend? Why, some ask, why would a good and Loving God let all this go on in the world? Did God leave us, or did mankind leave God by their disobedience to God? Yes, the latter is true—mankind left God by their disobedience to God.

God's original intent was for mankind to live on this earth without sin. He instructed man to replenish the earth, to subdue it (meaning to responsibly use its many resources), to have dominion over this planet (including the plants and animals), and to be fruitful and multiply (Genesis 1:28). Mankind was given authority on the earth by God Himself. However, there was one condition for living in peace on earth: not to sin. The condition was given to man through a single command. That specific command is found in Genesis 2:16-17 (KJV).

16. And the Lord God commanded the man, saying, "Of every tree of the garden, thou mayest freely eat." 17. "But the tree of the knowledge of good and evil, thou shall not eat of it; for in the day that thou eatest thereof, thou shall surely die."

This was the only command or law of God to man at that time, and it held the immense significance regarding life and death. As we observe in the next chapter of Genesis, mankind allowed himself to be deceived by the enemy Satan, and that allowed man's authority on this earth to be transferred to Satan and for sin to be introduced into the world.

So, why was this violation/sin of man so horrific? The answer, in simple terms, is because for the first time, man, by his actions, said to God, "I do not trust you." By his actions, man said to God, "There is someone or something else I trust more than you." Man, through this sin, put a Satanic, Devilish spirit above God. This act of man was high treason and represented man turning his back on God.

So then, how can man overcome this act of disobedience and treason? Does God forgive this foul act of mankind?

So many people have asked, "Why was this act of eating a fruit from a tree so terrible? It seems like it could have even been just a simple mistake." But what Adam and Eve did was much more than just eating a forbidden fruit. They disobeyed what was God's only law at the time. You see, when God created this earth, He did not just put man on the earth to live here; He gave man dominion over this earth and everything that was here. God gave man the status: *god of this earth*. And when God gave man that dominion and authority, He did not intend for man to give it away. Yet, that is exactly what man did by allowing himself to be deceived by God's enemy, Satan, and relinquishing man's authority and control to Satan.

God, in His ultimate and great wisdom, knew that when He created man and gave man authority over the earth, man would be a free thinker, capable of making independent decisions, because man was made in God's own image. God, as our Father and example, is also an independent and free thinker. This likeness to God includes the gift of free will and independent thought for mankind.

While man did not have the moral right (according to God's Divine will or desire), man did have the legal right to transfer his authority over the earth to Satan. When man sinned by disobeying God's command not to eat from the forbidden tree, authority was handed over to Satan, and he became the god of this world. (See 2 Corinthians 4:4.) The term "god of this world" refers to a lowercase "g" god. It signifies that after Adam's or man's sin, Satan gained the legal right to establish a world system characterized by sin, wrongdoing, and actions contrary to the goodness of God the Father.

Yes, God knew that man would make mistakes and sin. Just like any of us as parents, we feel saddened and disappointed when our children make mistakes. But as loving parents, what do we do when our children make bad choices? We certainly don't abandon or completely leave them. No loving parent would do that. Instead, parents try to help their children, have conversations with them, and teach them valuable lessons in trust and forgiveness, hoping that they will learn from their mistakes.

This is exactly what our Father, God, did for us. He did not leave us alone. He provided us a way out, a Redeemer and Savior named Jesus Christ, who came to save us from our sins.

Who Is Jesus?

Many people in the world today do not know who Jesus is and do not believe in Him. The main purposes of this book are, first, to share with you the revelation and reality of Hell; and, second, to help you understand that Jesus is real and that He is the only way to stay out of Hell and reach Heaven. There have been songs sung, movies made, books and poems written about Jesus to convey His reality. However, the only thing that will truly convince you of His existence is to have a personal relationship with Him. This involves getting to know Him through His Word, the Bible, and inviting Jesus into your heart.

In the Bible, Jesus is referred to by many names. But most important, to truly understand who Jesus is, you must recognize that He is part of the Godhead, a triune (three-part) being. There is God the Father, God as Jesus, and God the Holy Spirit. Although there is but one God, He functions in three distinct ways: as the Father, the Son (Jesus), and the Holy Spirit. This triune Divine being has always existed and preexisted. This is what God was referring to in Genesis 1:26 when He said, "Let Us … make man in Our image." The phrase "Let Us" refers to God in His threefold Divine nature.

God knew that man was imperfect when He made him, and God knew that man would sin. Jesus' primary role as a member of the Godhead was to be man's Redeemer, serving as a substitute for man's sin, and to be man's Savior from eternal damnation in Hell. God Himself came to this earth in the form of a flesh-and-blood man, taking the form of Jesus, in order to rescue mankind from the impending doom of Hell. When Jesus came to the earth, He was fully God while also being fully human, taking on a physical form.

There are numerous Divine names and titles ascribed to Jesus in order to demonstrate His Divine nature and His position as a member of the Godhead. Let me share just a few of these names mentioned in the Bible. Jesus is referred to as God and is indeed God Himself (John 1:1, 2, 14; Philippians 2:6-11; John 10:30, 38; John 12:45; Colossians 1:15; Matthew 1:23; Isaiah 7:13-14). Jesus is known as Immanuel, which means "God with us" (Matthew 1:23 KJV). He is called Lord and Lord of All (Luke 19:34; Acts 10:36). Jesus is recognized as the Son of God (Romans 1:4). He is described as Wonderful, Counselor, Mighty God, Everlasting Father, and Prince of Peace (Isaiah 9:6-7). Jesus is referred to as the Holy One of God (Mark 1:24) and as Lord and Savior (2 Peter 3:2). He is identified as the Alpha and Omega, the Beginning and the End, the First and the Last (Revelation 22:13). Jesus is called the Word of God (John 1:1, 2; Revelation 19:13) and the King of Kings and Lord of Lords (Revelation 19:16). There are many more titles given to describe Jesus in the Bible, and I encourage you to explore and discover them for yourself.

How Did Jesus Come to Us?

After mankind's act of disobedience and sin, it might have seemed logical for God to leave humanity in that sinful state, left to our own devices. Yet, God did not abandon us. Instead, out of His enduring Love for mankind, God provided a way for man to be delivered from our sinful state. God could not disregard the transgressions of man, but He also wanted to offer an alternative to eternal separation from Him. Divine justice required that the penalty for man's sin be paid, but mankind itself was not capable of paying that price. A Divine substitute was necessary to bear the cost of man's sin. Only God Himself could fulfill that role, and thus came the substitute and sacrifice … Jesus.

I reiterate, the sole solution for mankind's transgression was a future Savior and Redeemer known as Immanuel (God with us) or Jesus the Christ. While it would take thousands of years from the initial act of transgression by man to the physical appearance of Jesus on earth, God foretold the coming of the Savior in Genesis 3:15 (KJV): "And I will put enmity between thee and the woman, and between thy seed and her seed; it shall bruise thy head, and thou shall bruise his heel."

In this verse, God reveals His plan for a coming Messiah. This One, the seed of a woman, would be born through supernatural means and would set mankind free from the bondage of sin. The phrase "bruising the head" signifies the breaking of Satan's lordship or rule, as understood in Eastern languages. Through Jesus' sacrificial death on the cross, His burial, and resurrection, Satan's dominion over man was broken. Jesus stepped in as our substitute, taking the blame for us all. Now, for salvation, all we need to do is confess Jesus as our Lord and Savior and believe in His sacrifice, death, and resurrection. How great is our God for loving us so much that He did all that for us even though we did not earn or deserve it.

Why Did Jesus Come to Die for Us?

An anonymous quote wisely observed, "The two most important days of your life are when you were born and when you find out why." I wholeheartedly agree with this profound statement, but I would like to add a third significant day or event. It is the day or the moment when you get saved and accept Jesus as your Lord and Savior. Discovering why you were born and accepting Jesus as your Lord and Savior can be the same event, occurring on the same day. This event, also known as the Second Birth or the Born-Again Experience, is the reason why we are here on this earth, and is why Jesus came to die for mankind.

What I am about to share with you is undeniably the most crucial lesson in this book. In fact, it may be the most significant lesson you will ever learn. While it may appear too simple for some and too challenging to comprehend for others, it ultimately boils down to your willingness to receive and believe it. You see, no one, not even God Himself, can force you to believe something you don't want to believe. You alone possess the freedom of will and the power to make choices.

I simply ask you to consider the profound truth that it was God Himself, in the form of human flesh Jesus, who came to this earth with the purpose of saving mankind from the consequences of their sin nature. Without God's boundless Love and His gracious gift, humanity was destined for eternal death due to their inherent sinfulness. And as much as we may want to or think we can, we cannot save ourselves. We are in need of a Savior, and that Savior is none other than Jesus, who represents God's gracious gift to humanity.

Why Jesus came to die for us helps to answer the age-old questions: "Why are we on the earth?" and "What is the purpose of my life?" When we are born again and accept Jesus as our Lord and Savior, we enter into a personal relationship with Him. This relationship involves spending time with God in prayer, enjoying the blessings He has bestowed on us in this earthly life, and cherishing the quality time we spend with Him.

It also entails learning more about Him by reading His Word, the Bible. The Bible provides us with a wealth of insights and comprehension about why Jesus came to die for mankind. Among the many messages and teachings in the Bible, I believe there are three key reasons why Jesus came to die for us, which can be found in the Book of Mark 16:9-18 (AMPC).

I encourage you to invest time in reading, studying, and meditating on the Scriptures below.

9. Now Jesus, having risen [from death] early on the first day of the week, appeared first to Mary Magdalene, from whom He had driven out seven demons. 10. She went and reported it to those who had been with Him, as they grieved and wept. 11. And when they heard that He was alive and that she had seen Him, they did not believe it. 12. After this, He appeared in a different form to two of them as they were walking [along the way] into the country. 13. And they returned [to Jerusalem] and told the others, but they did not believe them either. 14. Afterward He appeared to the Eleven [apostles themselves] as they reclined at the table; and He reproved and reproached them for their unbelief (their lack of faith) and their hardness of heart, because they had refused to believe those who has seen Him and looked at Him attentively after He had risen [from

death]. 15. And He said to them, "Go into all the world and preach and publish openly the good news (the Gospel) to every creature [of the whole human race]." 16. "He who believes [who adheres to and trusts in and relies on the Gospel and Him Whom it sets forth] and is baptized will be saved [from the penalty of eternal death]; but he who does not believe [who does not adhere to and trust in and rely on (the Gospel) and Him Whom it sets forth] will be condemned." 17. "And these attesting signs will accompany those who believe: in My name they will drive out demons; they will speak in new languages;" 18. "They will pick up serpents; and [even] if they drink anything deadly, it will not hurt them; they will lay their hands on the sick, and they will get well."

Taken from the above text of Scripture are the **three key reasons why Jesus died for mankind and rose again for us.** I will list them here and discuss them in more detail below.

(1) Jesus died and rose again so that mankind will believe in Him and the Gospel, the Good News, that Jesus brings, so that mankind can be saved.

(2) Jesus died and rose again so that those who believe and are saved will share the Gospel, the Good News, with others so that they too can be saved.

(3) Jesus died and rose again so that those who have been saved will now recognize that, because of their salvation in Christ Jesus, they now have authority over the enemy, Satan, and his demonic forces. Believers can exercise their authority in Christ to overcome the power of darkness.

These three reasons highlight the significance of Jesus' death and resurrection for mankind's belief, salvation, and authority over the enemy. Now let's delve into these reasons in more detail.

Key Reason One

Jesus died for mankind and rose again so that mankind will believe in Him and the Gospel, the Good News, that Jesus brings, so that mankind can be saved.

The Scripture verses in Mark 16:9-14 depict the period immediately after Jesus has risen from the dead (His resurrection). Following His crucifixion on the cross at Calvary, His death, and His descent into Hell, where He defeated the enemy Satan, He physically came back on earth for many to witness. This time period marked the most significant event in human history, as Jesus' sacrificial act of dying, descending into Hell, and rising from the dead altered the course of human existence. For, without this redemptive act of God through Jesus Christ, mankind would not have a pathway to salvation.

After Jesus' resurrection, He returned to the earth to reveal Himself first to a small group of followers, including both men and women, who had believed in Him as the Messiah. These followers had walked and talked with Him and had been witnesses to His remarkable earthly ministry. As part of Jesus' ministry, they had witnessed Him perform miracles, such as healing the sick, giving sight to the blind, walking on water, raising people from the dead, and many others.

Among Jesus' followers, He had twelve male disciples who held a special position in His inner circle and were closer to Him than any other human beings throughout His three-year ministry on earth. These disciples were the original twelve men called to follow Jesus and be part of His earthly ministry. However, this number was later reduced to eleven due to the betrayal and death of one disciple named Judas Iscariot.

At the end of Jesus' earthly ministry, some of His followers witnessed His crucifixion and saw Him being hung on the cross by Roman soldiers. The eleven disciples, filled with fear, went into hiding, concerned that they too would face capture and death for their association with Jesus. It is important to note that none of these followers had ever witnessed a person being crucified (hung, beaten, and tormented on a cross), dying, and then coming back to life, walking and talking on earth as a normal human being. Despite Jesus' previous prophesies and teachings that He would be crucified, die, and rise again, there was much disbelief among His followers. Many struggled to comprehend how such a thing could be possible.

Even today, Jesus' death and resurrection remain challenging concepts for many to understand and believe. That is why *faith and cultivating a spiritual relationship with God through Jesus Christ* are essential aspects of being a Christian. These elements help us overcome doubt and embrace the profound truth of Jesus' sacrifice and victory over death.

After His resurrection, Jesus first appeared to Mary Magdalene, one of His loyal female followers. Although not much is known about Mary Magdalene's background, it is clear from the Bible that she was a dedicated and loyal follower of Jesus. Perhaps her devotion stemmed from the fact that Jesus had previously helped and healed her by casting out demonic spirits from her during His earthly ministry. (See Luke 8:2.) Having had that profound experience with

Jesus, she believed in Him wholeheartedly, and when she saw the risen Jesus she knew He was real.

As the first witness to see the risen Jesus, Mary Magdalene eagerly shared the news with others. She had no hesitation telling others that she had encountered the living Jesus once again, confirming His resurrection to those around her. When Mary Magdalene went to inform Jesus' disciples and close followers about her encounter with the risen Jesus, they initially did not believe her. Their doubts are understandable! Having witnessed Jesus' crucifixion and death, they must have been wondering, "How can He possibly be alive?" Yet He was very much alive and back among them! This miraculous event struck at the very heart of Christian faith and belief.

The *essence of a Christian's faith* lies in the understanding that Jesus willingly died for the sins of humanity and triumphantly rose again, with the offer that we may be saved if only we choose to believe in Him.

Before Jesus died and was raised from the dead, mankind did not have the opportunity to be saved or born again under God's *new covenant of grace*. The concept of salvation and being born again is intricately tied to accepting and believing in the death and resurrection of Jesus Christ, as well as in acknowledging Him as one's Lord and Savior. In the Book of Romans 10:9-10 (KJV), it is stated:

9. That if thou shalt confess with thy mouth the Lord Jesus, and shall believe in thine heart that God hath raised him from the dead, thou shall be saved. 10. For with the heart man believeth unto righteousness; and with the mouth confession is made unto salvation.

It is worth noting that the disciples who walked with and followed Jesus, witnessing the miracles He performed, were not saved. Why not? Because at the time of His earthly ministry, Jesus had not yet died and risen from the dead. Before Jesus was resurrected, He had not yet paid the price for mankind's sins. The redemptive actions of Jesus, including His suffering on the cross, death, descent into Hell, and resurrection were the necessary price for mankind's transgressions. No one could be saved before Jesus accomplished these events.

It was only after these events were completed that humanity's salvation became possible. Although initially surprised by Jesus' resurrection and return, once the disciples saw Jesus, they remembered His promise to return, and they then believed in Him as their Lord and Savior. It was then, after Jesus' resurrection and the disciples' acceptance of Jesus as their Lord and Savior, that they were saved. The message to the rest of the world is to believe in Jesus and accept Him as your Lord and Savior, and you too will be saved.

Key Reason Two

Jesus died and rose again so that those who believe and are saved will share the Gospel, the Good News, with others so that they too can be saved.

After the disciples had accepted Jesus as their Lord and Savior, Jesus commanded them to go into the world and preach the Gospel to every creature, to the entire human race (Mark 16:15). This command is not just for the disciples, but for all Believers. It signifies that God has given us humans an important life purpose.

First, our primary purpose is to know Jesus and receive Him as our Lord and Savior. Second, we are called to share Him with others.

You don't need to be a preacher or to have any special gifts, talents, licenses, or degrees to share Jesus with the world; you just have to have a willing heart or desire to share with other people what you have personally experienced in your relationship with Jesus.

Yes, you read that right. You don't have to be a trained preacher or minister to share God's Word and the Good News of Jesus. While having some formal spiritual training can be beneficial, it is not a requirement for sharing Jesus with others.

Sharing the message of Jesus often involves sharing your personal testimony of how God has worked in your life. It is about telling others how your relationship with God has transformed you and made a difference in your life. As you engage in sharing Jesus and the Word of God with a few people, the more comfortable and confident you will become sharing Him with many others. You will find that God, through the Holy Spirit, will guide and empower you, giving you the words to speak.

No matter what your profession or calling in life may be, you can share your experience of Jesus and make an impact on those around you.

Now, you may be thinking, *I don't want to be a preacher,* or, *I have not been called to be in ministry.* That's fine. Like I said, being a preacher or being in ministry is not a requirement for sharing Jesus, and it may be different from sharing your personal experience of Who Jesus is.

In my case, I never aspired to be a minister either, but once I got saved, I just liked talking to others about my relationship with God. However, later in life, God had different plans for me. After pursuing my personal dreams of being a military officer, working in business, and practicing law, God called me into ministry. While ministry is a wonderful calling, there are many other great professions and callings in life as well. Yet, what is so amazing is that God allows us to share the Gospel of Jesus no matter what profession we are in. Again, it all comes back to our willingness to do it.

No matter what your profession or vocation is in life, once you are saved and born again, you have a calling and ability to share the message of Jesus. This is what ministry is all about, and every Believer in Jesus has the capacity to minister to others. You can do it. However, be prepared, as fear is often the biggest obstacle to sharing Jesus. Fear, in this context, refers to the doubts and insecurities that Satan will try to instill in you to prevent you from speaking up. Satan does not want the world to know about the power of God and the name of Jesus, as it weakens his dominance in this world. But you can overcome that fear by praying to God daily for a spirit of boldness. He will grant you the strength to say what you need to say in any situation.

I can tell you from personal experience that fear comes from all directions. My mind gets bombarded with thoughts about what people will think or say about me. Will people think I am weird or crazy? Maybe I will say the wrong thing or won't know the answers. However, God has shown me through His Word and my time spent in prayer and listening to His voice that He is always with me, cares about me, and will provide everything I need to succeed in life. This includes giving me the right words to be a good witness for Him.

You know, it is common for everyone who has shared the message of Jesus to have doubts and insecurities at some point. But an amazing thing about God is that He does not expect us to be perfect in our witness. What he desires is for us to be willing to step out in faith, and He will assist us with the right words to say. God understands that we may make mistakes, and that is why He is always there for us. We can trust and rely on Him completely. It is not our own abilities that carry us through the daily challenges of life, but rather God's grace and mercy that get us through every single time.

There are many examples in the Bible where God has spoken to certain people and asked them to do things that they felt unprepared or unequipped for. One of the most prominent examples is Moses in the Old Testament, specifically in the Book of Exodus.

Moses was born to a Hebrew mother but was abandoned and found by another woman, who happened to be the daughter of the powerful Egyptian ruler known as Pharaoh. Thus, Moses was raised in a privileged and influential environment. However, when Moses reached adulthood, he witnessed an Egyptian beating a Hebrew man. Filled with anger over this mistreatment of one of his fellow Hebrews, Moses killed the Egyptian. Afraid for his own life, Moses fled Egypt to avoid punishment and the wrath of Pharaoh. It is important to note that during these times, the Hebrew people had been enslaved and oppressed by the Egyptians for hundreds of years.

In Exodus 3:9-11 (NIV), it was God Himself who spoke to Moses, saying, "And now the cry of the Israelites has reached me, and I have seen the way the Egyptians are oppressing them. So now, go, I am sending you to Pharaoh to bring my people the Israelites out of Egypt." But Moses responded to God, expressing his doubts and questioning his own ability. He asked, "Who am I, that I should go to Pharaoh and bring the Israelites out of Egypt?" Moses did not want to do what God wanted him to do and continued to give God excuses for why he could not do it and was not the right choice. Moses, in essence, was saying to God, "Why me? You got it wrong, God. You made a mistake." Can you imagine telling the Omnipotent (All-Powerful and All-Knowing) God, that He, the Creator of the Universe, got it wrong?

If you don't know the story of Moses, I encourage you to read it. Despite facing difficulties and hardships, Moses ultimately did what God commanded. When we trust God, like Moses did, we will win and ultimately have the victory. I use this story as an example of how most people are today, even those who claim to believe in God. People make all kinds of excuses about why they cannot obey God and why they cannot share the message of Jesus with others. It's important to recognize that whatever your excuses are, they are just that—excuses. Yet, I want to remind you again that one of our life purposes is to share the Gospel of Jesus. While most people in this world cannot see that or understand why, I assure you, one day it will become clear.

Our Time to Share

As brothers in the faith, Gary and I felt compelled to write this book as a means of sharing the Gospel of Jesus. Certainly, we've had the privilege of sharing Jesus with others in different ways before writing this book. Personally, I have talked to friends, family, and sometimes complete strangers about Jesus and the importance of accepting Him as Lord and Savior. I have witnessed to others in churches, grocery stores, on the street, and various other places. Gary tells the story of how he runs into strangers in the parking lot of a hardware store and ends up in a conversation about the Lord Jesus and salvation. Of course, there were times earlier in our lives when we were not so ready and willing to talk about matters of faith to anyone. I am thinking that many of you who are reading this book now were at such a place in your life once. Many of you are likely there right now. So, what led to the transformation that made us now more willing to share about our God and Lord Jesus? *Simply put, experiencing Him firsthand for ourselves!*

Now, as biological brothers, Gary and I have much the same background and upbringing. We both went to church as young boys and even joined and became members of our local Baptist church. While we both were active members in the church (I even sang in the youth choir), neither of us fully understood the importance of accepting Jesus as our Lord and Savior. It was like we were just going through the motions and doing what we thought we were supposed to do.

In my case, I believed I was generally doing the right things and considered myself a good person, but even so, I always felt like something was missing. I was a church member, yet I found myself engaging in sinful behavior such as partying, drinking alcohol, and having premarital sex. I was torn between enjoying these sinful actions while also hating the fact that I was sinning. As the younger brother, I saw many of the same patterns in Gary's life. In fact, I ended up repeating many of the mistakes he made.

So, you might ask, what changed or helped us? And please know, we will never profess to be flawless or perfect people. It is through the grace of God that we have been able to progress over time and understand more clearly who God is. These positive changes in our lives were not immediate, but took time. It was only by the patience and grace of God that we were spared dying in an unsaved state. It saddens us to think many, just like us, may be headed down a path of danger, death, and destruction and not even realize it. It was through a journey filled with time and many difficulties that God showed us the truth that, if not for Him, we would not have made it out.

Through our individual journeys and challenging times, God revealed who He really is to both Gary and me. At different times and in different circumstances, we each made the decision to invite Jesus into our heart and be saved. We committed ourselves to Him and began taking our relationship with Him more seriously. It was then that our lives began to change for the better. You can experience this transformation too, by asking Jesus to come into your heart right now.

While the changes Gary and I have experienced have occurred at different times and in different ways—after all, we are two different people going through very different life experiences—a huge part of that change for us was to begin sharing our experience with Jesus with others. The enemy Satan will do his best to keep us all from sharing Jesus because he knows that will defeat his own dominance on this earth.

This book, as you know, is a means of sharing God's Word through Jesus Christ. We now believe and understand that Gary's experience of going to Hell was a way for God to emphasize that our earthly lives have an expiration date and will come to an end, and that Hell is a real place that awaits those who do not make the right choice of accepting Jesus.

You may have heard stories about Hell before and not taken them seriously or dismissed them as some kind of fable or myth. I don't know what you have heard or who you have heard it from, but we want you to know that Hell is a real place. The smartest decision you will ever make is to believe that and choose Heaven over Hell.

Key Reason Three

Jesus died and rose again so that those who have been saved will now recognize that, because of their salvation in Christ Jesus, they now have authority over the enemy, Satan, and his demonic forces. Believers can exercise their authority in Christ to overcome the power of darkness.

Jesus died and rose again for mankind so that Christians can know that they have authority over the enemy Satan.
(See Mark 16:16-18, Luke 10:18-19.)

"Submit yourselves therefore to God. Resist
the devil, and he will flee from you."
—James 4:7 (KJV)

This third key reason may be the most difficult for most people, including Christians, to grasp and fully embrace. We have often been taught and heard that Satan, *this big powerful being,* is too strong for us mere mortals and that we should live in fear of him. However, this belief is far from the truth. As someone who has accepted Jesus as your Lord and Savior, you possess authority over the enemy Satan. Undoubtedly, what Satan wants every human being to believe is that he has authority over us. He wants us to believe that so he can continue to maintain control over us.

But as I have shared, the great news is that if you have accepted Jesus as your Lord and Savior, you now have authority over Satan, his kingdom, and all of his cohorts on this earth.

This third reason for Jesus' death and resurrection is our *authority*. Understanding our authority is crucial for us to fully access the many blessings and promises God has provided for us in His Word, the Bible. These promises include health, safety, peace, prosperity, and long life on earth, among many others. Unless we recognize that these promises from God are truly ours, then the Devil will try to convince us that they are not.

To fully benefit from these promises, you must first know your authority over Satan. So, what is this authority, and why is it so significant?

Authority, translated from the Greek word "exousia," encompasses the concepts of freedom and legal rights. The New Testament portrays exousia in a number of ways, always consistent in the acknowledgment that there is no authority except from God (Romans 13:1, John 19:11). The term "exousia" first describes the freedom of God to act (Luke 15:5, Acts 1:7) and, second, signifies the power and authority given to Jesus Christ by the Father God (Matthew 28:18, John 10:18, 17:2).

Derived from this Greek word "exousia," authority is the power or ability given to us by God Himself because of our relationship with Jesus Christ. It is not power or ability that we earned or deserve, but rather a free gift from God bestowed on us when we accept Jesus as our Lord and Savior.

There is a profound distinction between God-given authority and one's own personal physical power or might. Satan, the enemy, does not possess authority. Satan only possesses certain abilities that are not divine and not given by God. Satan is referred to as the god of this world (2 Corinthians 4:4), indicating that he is the small "g" god of this world system. This world system represents the ways of the world that are separate from Almighty God.

The Devil/Satan and this world system seek to dominate, control, and exert their influence over us. These abilities lie within Satan's dominion and control. Some of the things under Satan's dominion include sickness and disease, depression, sadness, death, strife, anger, conflict, war, storms, and dangerous weather patterns, to name a few.

God wants you to know that as a born-again Believer in Jesus Christ, you possess authority over the enemy Satan and all the ploys he can bring against you. In Mark 16:16-18 (KJV), God outlines examples of the authority given to us through Christ Jesus.

16. He that believeth and is baptized shall be saved; but he that believeth not shall be damned. 17. And these signs shall follow them that believe; In my name shall they cast out devils; they shall speak with new tongues; 18. They shall take up serpents; and if they drink any deadly thing, it shall not hurt them; they shall lay hands on the sick, and they shall recover.

In verse 16, we are shown that Believers have authority over the enemy of eternal death. That means you have authority and power over Hell. By accepting Jesus, you are saved, but if you refuse to believe and deny His existence, you will be damned. In doing so, you are in fact giving yourself over to the Devil and facing an eternal damnation from which there is no way out.

In verse 17, God grants Believers authority and power over the Devil and his demonic forces during our time on earth. While these words may be difficult to understand and harder to believe, your future and your eternal life depend on you believing this and acting on it. When I first read this verse, I did not fully comprehend or believe it either. But, when you begin to experience a life with God, you will find that there is nothing the Devil can do to you. Satan is doing everything in his power to prevent you from discovering this truth—your authority.

What's also amazing here is that God tells us that He has bestowed on Believers a special gift known as tongues. When a person accepts Jesus, they can receive the baptism of the Holy Spirit, accompanied by the ability to speak in tongues. Speaking in tongues simply refers to a Heavenly language of prayer and praise that allows you to speak directly with God. It grants you greater power and understanding of who God is and strengthens your relationship to Him.

Last, in verse 18, God informs Believers that we have authority over sickness and disease. The world is filled with so many deadly elements that seek to harm and destroy us. The Word of God uses metaphorically the terms "serpents" and "drink any deadly thing" to represent things that are specifically designed to cause harm and potentially lead to death. However, as a Believer who invokes the name of Jesus, you can exercise authority over these adversaries, such as sickness, disease, and even death itself.

You see, God never intended for mankind to be plagued by sickness and disease. These afflictions are a result of the *curse* that entered the earth through Satan during the transgression and fall of man. But, thank God, there is a way out, and that way is through Jesus.

During the early stages of the COVID pandemic, Gary was diagnosed with the disease. Given his age, he fell into the high-risk category, and many others were going to the hospital and even died. Gary was sent to the hospital with difficulty breathing and a lung infection. The early words from some of the attending medical experts were not very encouraging. One doctor said he did not think Gary would survive.

In that critical moment, the most crucial action we took was to exercise our authority and continually declare Gary's healing, saying aloud to the Devil that Gary will live and not die. We continued to praise God for his healing and, in a few days, Gary was well and out of the hospital, healed of the virus and its symptoms.

Some might dismiss this extraordinary recovery as just a coincidence, but we know the truth. It was the power of God at work, along with Gary's exercise of his authority over the enemy virus that had attacked his body. While we are thankful for the medical support and science, we give God the glory and praise for Gary's healing.

Authority in This Earth Realm

As we discussed in a previous chapter, God originally intended for man to have dominion over the earth (Genesis 1:26). However, due to the tragic event of Adam's sin and transgression, Satan acquired a legal right to operate on this earth, ushering in spiritual darkness and all that opposes God's will.

This legal right was stolen by Satan because Adam yielded and succumbed to Satan's lies and deception. But although Satan has the legal right to operate on this earth, he does not and will never have the moral right to dominate the earth or mankind unless mankind gives him that right. His time to operate on this earth is limited and will eventually come to an end. (See Revelation 20:1-3, 9-10.)

Satan's primary means of overpowering humanity is through lies and deception. He wants people to believe he is more powerful than Almighty God. Sadly, so many people are duped and taken in by Satan's lies and manipulations. Often, we may think we are being clever and getting away with something, when in reality, it is the Devil's ploy to get us to do something that is wrong.

For example, imagine you are walking through a department store in a mall, and you spot a small yet valuable item on display. Suddenly, a voice in your head says, "Put it in your pocket and walk out. No one will know." You do it and get outside the doors without anyone seeing you. You now think you are so smart because you got away with it. But, no, you are not smart, because the Devil just deceived you into doing wrong, and someday you will be accountable for it. Don't fall for these deceptions.

Just because Satan has the right to operate on this earthly plane does not mean he has authority over man unless man gives it to him. One of the greatest gifts God has bestowed on us is our spiritual authority over the Devil and his allies. Spiritual authority is not some magic pill you take every morning when you get up. You receive it by accepting Jesus as your Lord and Savior and then choosing to use that authority over the Devil and against the Devil's attacks against you.

An example that helps illustrate how Godly authority works is that of a traffic police officer standing at an intersection when the traffic light is out or during some major event, such as a sporting event or a music concert, where there is a huge volume of traffic. The officer stands at the intersection and simply holds up their hands, and the traffic comes to a stop. Now, why does the traffic stop? Is it because the officer possesses superhuman strength like Superman that he can hold back those powerful vehicles? No, of course not. It's because the drivers of the vehicles recognize the authority vested in the officer by the municipal or state government to regulate traffic.

Our God-given spiritual authority operates in a similar manner. It is not dependent on our physical abilities or our mortal strength or aptitudes. Instead, it is the authority we possess through Jesus Christ that empowers us to overcome the will of the Devil and prevent him from overpowering us.

I remember many years ago when my wife and I were on a business trip to Tampa, Florida. After our business was done, we had a little time left so we decided to visit some relatives in the nearby city of St. Petersburg. We were excited to see our two very special aunts, Mattie and Lillie. As we talked and visited for over an hour, our aunts brought up the idea of having a family reunion. They pointed out that we had a large extended family with relatives scattered all across the country, yet we had never organized a reunion. They suggested that my wife and I take the lead in coordinating this long-awaited gathering.

Initially, I thought of every reason why we could not do it, from not having the time, to living too far away from the proposed reunion location. However, our aunts, who were getting older, insisted we do it. They were so persuasive, we finally agreed. After a year of extensive planning, the highly anticipated reunion weekend arrived.

The response was overwhelming, with over 350 family members showing up. The first night was the reunion reception inside a very nice hotel. However, the second day was the family outing, picnic, and lots of food and games. This family picnic was to be held outside in a park in Tallahassee, Florida. Tallahassee is known for its springtime showers, and rain had been predicted for that whole day.

I remember praying about the situation and reminding God about all the time and expense that had gone into the planning of this day. And I remember the Holy Spirit speaking to me in response, saying in a stern voice, "Use your authority. Take authority over this rain today." I did not fully understand at the time what "take authority" meant, as I had never done it before. Yet, I made up my mind to obey and act on the instruction given to me.

Early that morning, I stepped outside, gazed up at the sky and said with conviction, "In the name of Jesus, it will not rain today on our picnic." And, sure enough, praise God, it did not rain! It was a beautiful day all day, and we all had an amazing time together. The only rain that day came later that night, well after everyone had gone home. You might say this was just another coincidence, but I know it was the power of God operating in this earth realm as I used my authority. Since that time, I have successfully used my authority over storms and other bad weather in the same way. And not just over the weather, but in other areas of my life as well. As I have now personally experienced many times, God's Word works!

I know you are probably wondering, "Can this be real? Is it biblical?" Well, Jesus showed us by example that when He was on earth in human form, He exercised authority over natural elements. And if it was right for Jesus, it is right for us Believers who confess Jesus as our Lord and Savior. In Mark 4:39 (KJV), Jesus rebuked the wind and the sea during a great storm, demonstrating His authority by saying, "Peace, be still." Miraculously, the wind ceased and there was a great calm. Additionally, in Mark 11:13, 14, 20 (AMPC), Jesus spoke to a fig tree, declaring, "No one ever again shall eat fruit from you." The very next morning Jesus and His disciples witnessed the fig tree withered from its roots.

God is showing mankind that we are specially made. We are fearfully and wonderfully created in His image, with the power to have dominion over this earth. That dominion includes dominance over the enemy, the Devil, and his hostile forces. It also includes dominance over natural forces that would harm or adversely affect us. Remember, the spiritual authority that God has given us is not always tangible or visible, but it is real and effective, if only we use it. But we can only use it after we first willingly submit to God and His Word. James 4:7 makes it clear: "Submit yourselves therefore to God. Resist the devil, and he will flee from you." Notice that this does not say the Devil might flee, but that he *will flee* from you. This is the authority we possess. Let's boldly use it in Jesus' name!

Conclusion

The title *Hell Alert* was inspired by Gary Murray's profound real-life experience of leaving his physical body, dying, and enduring the terrifying realm of Hell. Gary's encounter with Hell was not some dream or even a dreadful nightmare; it was a genuine death experience that Gary was not sure he would escape from. It was only through the Grace of God and Gary's acceptance of Jesus as his Lord and Savior on earth, before this death experience, that he was released from the clutches of Hell.

The purpose of this book is not to frighten you or to give you some emotional excitement or distress. It is simply to share with the world what God allowed Gary to experience. It serves as a reminder that Hell is a real place and that many have gone there, most unwillingly. Conversely, Heaven is also a real place, and our ultimate goal should be to enter its gates. Within the pages of this book, we present clear options: Choose life in Jesus Christ or face the alternative of eternal damnation in Hell.

If nothing else, let this book be the beginning of your journey to discover your reason for being on this earth. We pray that you come to realize that the answers lie in Almighty God, our Father, through our Lord Jesus Christ. If you have yet to embrace God as your Father and make Jesus your Lord and Savior, we implore you to do it now, before it is too late. You can make Jesus your Lord and Savior by simply confessing and believing the words on the next page, called the Prayer of Salvation.

Make Your Decision: Prayer of Salvation

Receive Jesus as Your Lord and Savior

If you have never made Jesus your Lord and Savior, now is the time to do so. This is the most important decision you will ever make. In His Word, God has made a profound promise to us:

"If thou shalt confess with thy mouth the Lord Jesus, and shalt believe in thine heart that God hath raised him from the dead, thou shalt be saved. For with the heart man believeth unto righteousness; and with the mouth confession is made unto salvation … For whosoever shall call upon the name of the Lord shall be saved."
—*Romans 10:9-10, 13 (KJV)*

By praying (out loud) the following simple prayer and genuinely believing it, you will be saved.

"Jesus, I recognize that I am a sinner. I repent and ask You to forgive me of my sins. I confess You, Jesus, as my Lord and Savior. I believe in my heart that You died for me and that God raised You from the dead. By faith in Your Word, I now believe that I am saved. I receive my salvation now. Thank You, Jesus, for saving me. In Jesus' name, Amen!"

Congratulations! You are now born again and have become a member of the Family of God. We encourage you to get a Bible and seek out a good church home where the Word of God is preached and taught. Being part of a community of Believers will enrich your understanding and strengthen your faith in God's Word.

About the Authors

Gary H. Murray is a veteran of the U.S. Marine Corps and served during the Vietnam War, where he sustained severe injuries and was awarded medals for valor, including the Purple Heart. Throughout his life, Gary has faced many challenges, but none as life-changing as his death experience, journeying  to Hell, and returning to share his profound encounter with the world. Now, driven by a deep passion for God, Gary's utmost desire is to effectively convey the goodness of God and the teachings of Jesus Christ to others in the best ways he can.

S. Charles Murray, Gary's younger brother, is a distinguished veteran of the U.S. Army and Army Reserves. He served for twenty-six years, culmi-  nating in the rank of Full Colonel before retiring. He served a tour in the Iraq War and received numerous military awards and accolades for his exemplary service. Charles has assumed various roles throughout his life, including minister, teacher, speaker, director, author, business owner, attorney, and judge. Despite his impressive achievements, he now regards his most significant mission to be the sharing of the Gospel of Jesus Christ.

www.ingramcontent.com/pod-product-compliance
Lightning Source LLC
Chambersburg PA
CBHW040148160726
48006CB00014B/1663